CREATING

A CULTURE OF

EXCELLENCE

CREATING A CULTURE

OF EXCELLENCE

Changing the World of Work One Person at a Time

WIL DAVIS

authorHOUSE™

1663 LIBERTY DRIVE, SUITE 200
BLOOMINGTON, INDIANA 47403
(800) 839-8640
WWW.AUTHORHOUSE.COM

First published by AuthorHouse 08/08/05

ISBN: 1-4208-6040-2 (sc)
ISBN: 1-4208-6041-0 (dj)

Library of Congress Control Number: 2005905112

Printed in the United States of America
Bloomington, Indiana

This book is printed on acid-free paper.

CONTENTS

Dedication   ix

Preface: Steve Bell   xiii
        Professor of Telecommunications
        Ball State University
        Former News Anchor of ABC's
        Good Morning America

Prologue: The Key to Organizational Excellence   xvii
Introduction: Why Are You Working?   1

Part I: Creating a Culture of Excellence
Chapter 1: A Framework that Works   13
Chapter 2: Stewardship   21
Chapter 3: Integrity   25
Chapter 4: Service   31
Chapter 5: Tolerance—Respect for the Individual   43
Chapter 6: Professionalism   49

Part II: Leadership within a Culture of Excellence
Chapter 7: High-Performance Leadership   55
Chapter 8: Vision   63
Chapter 9: Values   69
        Stewardship—It's All about People   70
        Integrity—Personal Example   72
        Service—Servant Leadership   75
        Tolerance—Respect for the Individual—Loving People   77
        Professionalism—Walking the Talk   79

Part III: Accountability—Keeping the Integrity of the Culture

Chapter 10: Accountability—Keeping the Culture   87

Chapter 11: Receiving Accountability   97

Chapter 12: Giving Accountability   103

Part IV: Practices of the Culture

Chapter 13: The Difference it Makes   115

Epilogue: Transforming Work—Transforming the World   125

DEDICATION

This book is dedicated to:

- The workers of the world. As a person builds a house, so the house builds the person. May you become a cathedral!

- My first and best teachers in life, my dad and mom, Earl C. and Martha H. Davis, and to my brothers and sisters who formed me by their love and encouragement. Sharon, Richard, Merribeth, and Gil—You are the best siblings any brother has ever had!

- My business partner and true friend, Ron Fauquher, and his wife, Cheryl. Without these dear friends and Ron's strength of character and competence, there would be no story to tell—no book to write. I am forever indebted to you both. Many THANKS!

- The entire team at Ontario Systems, who prove each day that work can be a blessing, not a curse, and that working together, we can change the world in a positive way

- My wife and best friend, Cindy, and our wonderful children. When we started the business, the kids were ages five, two, and one. With incredible strength and dedication, Cindy selflessly encouraged me to pursue building a business while she became the primary builder of our family. Her work can easily be judged an unqualified success! I can only hope to someday achieve her standards in my building project! To Jennifer, Steve, and Elizabeth and your wonderful spouses, I am so proud of your personal sense of vocation. You are a blessing to us and the primary legacy we will leave to the world.

"Whatever is true, whatever is noble, whatever is right, whatever is pure, whatever is lovely, whatever is admirable—if anything is excellent or praiseworthy—think about such things."

Philippians 4:8 (NIV)

PREFACE

Wil Davis is a man with a mission. He wants to change the world of work, one person at a time! But before you read this unique contribution to the literature of leadership and corporate culture, a warning label is appropriate:

> Warning: This book is dangerous to those whose self-image depends on executive perks or a reputation for knowing how to say "you're fired." If you are not careful, you will find your management assumptions, your psyche, and your self-image undermined by the hard-nosed logic and corporate success of a "preacher's kid" who is not afraid to preach a gospel of empowering others to maximize your bottom line.

In the interest of full disclosure, let the record show that I have known and admired Wil Davis since he first spoke to our senior telecommunications majors at Ball State University several years ago and shared some of the ideas in this book. For young men and women about to enter the workforce, he offered both wisdom and inspiration.

I also have a son-in-law who works for Ontario Systems. And in one of our first conversations, he said matter-of-factly that he is a better person as well as a better employee because of the corporate culture where he works.

In *Creating a Culture of Excellence*, Wil Davis argues that the most important asset a business has is its "intellectual capital." And the way to grow it is to help each employee turn his or her work time into "a positive, healthy, life-giving experience."

This book could not come at a more critical juncture in the evolution of corporate America. The culture of greed personified by CEO excesses and malfeasance has discredited the school of singular focus on "enhancing shareholder value" and the quarterly bottom line (too often fabricated, we now know). Yet in a world marketplace where corporate competitors can thrive outside the normal constraints of government regulation, what can a serious business leader or aspiring entrepreneur do?

Wil Davis makes no pretense of having all the answers. But he is a serious student of business management and leadership who openly draws from the ideas of others while fusing them with his own unique philosophy. And at its core is the belief that putting others first, and putting them in a work environment where they can thrive both personally and professionally, is the key to corporate success.

Wil makes no secret of the role that his personal spiritual journey plays in his business philosophy. The Statement of Corporate Philosophy he offers lifts up Jesus Christ as the ultimate example of a successful "organization guy." But rest assured that he separates church and state when it comes to testing the business concepts that emerge and holding them accountable to corporate performance. If you are ready to test the premise that "life is a gift, and our work a part of the gift," then you will be ready to have a dialogue with Wil over how best to put that gift to work.

To put this book into context, you need to look at the man and his own corporate balance sheet. Wil and his partner, Ron Fauquher, began their entrepreneurial dream in a garage. Today, Ontario Systems has more than 500 employees, healthy profits, and a best-in-class reputation in their computer software specialty area.

How do you make that happen? In this post-Enron era of corporate culture, you are forgiven if the word "stewardship" didn't come to mind. But Wil Davis would like to prove to you that a good corporate leader is a steward first, one who manages on behalf of the real owner. Ah, yes, the shareholder, you say. No, that's only partly right.

In fact, the key to organizational excellence is to realize that businesses have multiple stakeholders: investor/owners, employees, customers, vendors, even our communities. Being a good steward is to serve the best, long-term interests of all these people. And the best steward is someone able to balance the needs of the multiple stakeholders with the good of the business.

On the surface, this can sound like a feel-good bromide that would never survive the real corporate world. But when Wil Davis gets into the nitty-gritty of corporate leadership, the operative word is "accountability." And it is not a one-way street where only the employee is held accountable. On the contrary, creating a culture of excellence calls for a "360-degree appraisal process" in which all those in supervisory roles receive performance appraisals not only from those above them, but also from everyone they supervise.

In explaining and advocating this process, Wil offers one of the wonderful personal experiences that give meaning to this book. He tells how, as a young bank supervisor, he asked for assessments from those under him and got a litany of criticism, even about a particular pair of slacks he wore. After a weekend of agony, he went back to work determined to respond positively as best he could. Today, he is chairman of the board at that bank, and some of those critical employees are among his best friends.

Another example of the "tough love" required to build a culture of excellence has to do with confronting issues when they arise.

Many of us let problems fester rather than risk confrontation. But Wil Davis not only advocates being a proactive manager, he also offers specific guidelines for holding others accountable, up to and including termination.

Looking back at my own thirty-five years in broadcast journalism and now another dozen in education, it is tempting to hold both myself and others accountable in hindsight. If only I had approached the workforce with such wisdom and insight. If only some of the news executives and bureau chiefs I worked for had fostered a culture of excellence. During my eleven years as the news anchor on *Good Morning America*, I had more than a dozen producers and executive producers, each with their own ideas and idiosyncrasies.

But the truth is, many of my colleagues and I did a pretty good job much of the time in forging a workplace environment that gave us the joy and satisfaction of working together to do and be our best. It's just that we never thought to identify and articulate the theory and practice that produce, and then reproduce, the best that we can be.

Now, Wil Davis has done that for us. And for many of you it will be just in time to change your lives, and to help you change the lives of others by working toward a culture of excellence.

Steve Bell
Professor of Telecommunications
Ball State University
Former News Anchor of ABC's *Good Morning America*

PROLOGUE:
THE KEY TO ORGANIZATIONAL EXCELLENCE

The only truly unique, sustainable competitive advantage that any business has is in the unique, unduplicated intellectual capital of its people. Competitors can copy our existing products. Somebody will always find a cheaper source of unskilled labor. But no one can take away the creativity, initiative, diligence, and perseverance of our own team!

If that's true, and I believe it is, the real question for businesspeople around the globe is not so much about what is going on "out there" as what is going on "in here." Is anybody else relieved to know that we really don't always need to outsource our own work just to create a competitive advantage? Admittedly, there are certain elements of what some firms do that are very appropriately outsourced to other firms, which may or may not be in our country. Either through specialization or lower-cost resources, there are many circumstances where outsourcing can be appropriate. My instincts are, however, that we in American business have outsourced more than we needed to, and in many cases, more than we should have. The primary reason? Our own companies didn't create a corporate culture in which excellence in innovation and/or execution were the distinguishing characteristics of the company.

I live in a community that had two very large industry concentrations that provided economic vitality for many years. One industry was building manual transmissions for the automotive industry. The other industry was building the very large transformers that were used in the electrical distribution industry. Building manual transmissions for cars and trucks or very large electrical transformers for the wholesale power grid were great businesses when the technology was new and the markets were growing. But as those markets matured, and new technologies replaced large parts of the respective markets for manual transmissions or freight-train-sized transformers, these particular manufacturers simply continued to build what they had always built (with incremental improvements, of course), and they essentially failed to generate a competitive response to the "sea change" of challenges in their core markets. When abundance (growing markets) is replaced by scarcity (shrinking markets), the inevitable tension between various cost components of a manufactured product intensifies. As a major cost component, direct labor felt intense pressure to maintain jobs while accepting less generous compensation increases. With less than visionary leadership in both the major unions that represented labor as well as the company leadership, the relationship between labor and management at both of these major industries became notoriously acrimonious. (That we refer to the employees of these kinds of organizations by those two labels, "labor" and "management," is, in my opinion, symptomatic of a deeper cultural issue which we will address later in this book.) The big-picture problem of manufacturing products for which there was a diminishing market was lost to the battle between powerful stakeholders within the company who both insisted on doing exactly what they had always done. Today, one business is completely gone from our community, and the other continues to shrink. In essence, these companies were built on unique intellectual property, but it did not renew itself, and the businesses fell prey to voracious competition from other, lower-cost competitors. It is a very scary place to be as a businessperson when you realize that your only competitive advantage has been reduced to price!

What would it require for our businesses to build and sustain a unique competitive advantage based on the value-add of our team members? From both personal and corporate experience gained over the last twenty-five years, I have come to the conclusion that businesses, and business leaders in particular, need to reinvent themselves around value systems that work for both the individuals in the company and the company itself. Only by successfully engaging the whole persons with whom we work can we find the collective wisdom to build sustained commercial success. To me, that's the hallmark of a great corporate culture, and it's the goal toward which I aspire every day.

This book simply chronicles some of the lessons from my own experiences at work. Because it is a personal sharing, it may not map directly into your world; however, I'm hoping that you will find enough common ground to consider the merits and benefits of creating a corporate culture that breeds personal and organizational excellence.

We are still on the journey, so I cannot say that we have fully arrived. There will be many more twists and turns ahead, but I believe our foundation is strong, and with the competitive advantage we have with our team and its culture, I'm excited to meet those challenges and further enhance our competitive position. We're passionate about what we do! This book is about how we created, and how we sustain, that passion.

Enjoy!

wrd

INTRODUCTION:
WHY ARE YOU WORKING?

Most of us grow up with the assumption that we will go to work. Work seems to be the reason we exist—we go to school, we stay in school, we graduate from school, we go to more school, we graduate again—sometimes again and again—and if someone were to hazard a guess as to why we were doing all this, it would probably be because our culture teaches us that education leads to "better" work. In general, "better" in this case means better pay, better stability, and, in general, less physical work.

How about you? Why are you working? Go ahead—write down your top reasons—I'll wait. . . .

Let's compare those to the list I hear most often.

- *Make money*

- *Make money to provide for my family*

- *Make money to maintain our "standard of living"*—That's another phrase I want to challenge—standard of living is generally equated to a socioeconomic status. Is that how you are going to measure the quality of your living? Really? On your deathbed, you're going to want to reflect back and see that you had "all the toys," even though you will not be taking any of them with you?

- *Make money so I can retire so I won't have to work!* (Obviously, the goal of work is to not work!)

Next set—

- *I'd go nuts sitting around the house.*

- *I'd go nuts taking care of kids all day.*

- *I need to be doing something*—Hey, hey, hey—Believe it
  or not, we're getting closer with this one!

Next set—

- *I really believe what I'm doing is important—I'm involved in
  truly helping people, and I enjoy the challenge of contributing
  to solving the problems I face at work.*

In my experience, if you are in this last set, you are in the minority—
a blessed minority, but a minority nonetheless! Rarely do people
have this attitude about their work, and that includes people who
are often thought to be in the "helping" professions—doctors,
teachers, nurses, etc.

Let me ask another question—again, I'll wait while you jot down
an answer. What would you like work to be in your life?

I knew that would be hard. Most of us just haven't thought about it very
much. When we began working, it was simply expected. Everyone
goes to work when they become an adult. Without much thought, we
adopted the attitudes about work from those who were around us and
already doing the work (after all, they should be the experts—they've
been working longer than we have!) But when we found ourselves in
the world of work, many of us were greeted by a dramatic surprise.
Work was, let's be honest, a BIG disappointment.

This certainly reflects my personal experience. I remember graduating from undergraduate school and thinking about getting a job. Note: I did not say thinking about my life's work. I was young, married, tired of being a poor college student, and I was looking for a job—why? To make some money! (See reason #1 above!) It was not a morally wrong reason, but it wasn't very profound either. As I began searching for that first job, I thought about what kind of work environment I would like. Thinking about a work environment led me to think about cleanliness, air conditioning, dressing nicely every day, and working with people for whom cleanliness, air conditioning, and dressing nicely every day were also good things—after all, that would insure that they were nice people! So I went to work in a bank!

Sounds pretty naïve! It was! But, honestly, was your first job experience any better?

How about your commitment to the job? I know that my education left me with the distinct impression that to "get ahead," one needed to think about changing companies every two to four years, moving "up" the corporate ladder more quickly than opportunities within your own company were likely to become available. So, in all honesty, I took the job with a predisposition to leaving. My dissatisfaction was built-in. And sure enough, in three years, when I had an opportunity to change companies, I jumped at the opportunity. This time, I was jumping into a BIG company— General Motors—a stable company—a good pay raise—perhaps I was going to be much more committed to this company. After all, was there any limit to what I could do in a company that big? I was sure I would never run out of rungs on the ladder to climb!

A funny thing happened on the way to that spectacular career. I noticed what seemed to be a pattern. Just as had happened in my first job, after I had gotten through the major part of the learning curve, which took about nine months, and I had begun to exercise some genuine competency in the leading-edge research and development on which we were working, I began to notice that somewhat familiar, nagging feeling that I would bet many of you have felt, too. I was twenty-five years old, and I began to think about doing this job for the next forty years or so, when I would "retire," whatever that might mean. A forty-year career—and then what? Did it mean anything? Was there a purpose to spending my life "at work?"

Where did that idea come from—what made me wonder about the purpose to the years of my life—especially those years spent at work? Had this been the first time this pattern had happened, I might not have asked. But, it had happened twice in a row in my first two real-world experiences with work. And after only eighteen months on the second job, I found myself thinking about what my next "job" would be and whether or not it would be any more fulfilling.

Where do we get our ideas about work? In general, I suspect that they come from our families of origin. I'm sure that's true for me. For example, one of the things that bothered me most about work was how much time I wasted in the commute. It had never occurred to me that commute time was a "normal" part of work because my dad didn't commute. We lived next door to his primary place of work, and he had an office in our home. He worked lots of hours, but he never wasted any time in a thing as ridiculous as a commute! But when I went to work for GM, I found myself spending an hour and a half each day driving to and from the plant. Had I not ridden with my friend (and eventual business partner) both ways, I'm not sure I would have made it as long as I did! So, although I was not particularly conscious of the assumptions I had picked up about work from my dad, it was a good place to think about some of my other assumptions. By the way, my dad is a pastor—we lived next door to the church building, and we always had an office in the parsonage, as well.

What other assumptions had I adopted unconsciously about work from my father? Here was a man who never made much money, was on-call 24/7, worked every weekend and most evenings during the week, and loved it as much when he retired (due to health issues) after forty-three years of active duty as he did the day he first became a pastor. Was he always revered? Well, painfully and honestly, no. Was he always treated fairly? Again, people are people wherever you find them. So, people who treat others unfairly in the secular world also treat people unfairly in the sacred. In my experience, God is VERY gracious and does not often step in directly to set things straight—at least not immediately, so the answer to this question is, again, no. In spite of the realities of serving an organization made up of mostly volunteer leadership of varying caliber ability, the thing I observed was a deep and abiding commitment that kept him fulfilled in his work, even when the work was difficult.

It was about this time that I began to ponder the idea that perhaps only in the full-time pastoral ministry could someone find such happiness. Maybe that was it—some people were "special" and since God asked them to do their work, they received an unusual blessing from their work—abiding contentment. There was only one problem with this thought—my dad had preached against it his entire career! I had consciously learned—as opposed to unconsciously absorbing the other values—that from a God's-eye perspective, He desires that everyone find fulfillment in their lives—including their work lives. Besides, my dad had always told me, "if you're supposed to be in full-time, pastoral ministry, you won't be able to stay out of it." And for me, it was pretty obvious that I was NOT supposed to be in pastoral ministry! It has been very easy to avoid!

I found myself in a strange place. By most standards, I had a GREAT job! The pay was outstanding, the benefits were so good that we called our employer "Generous Motors," my work was on the cutting edge of technology at that time, and I was given assignments far beyond what was merited in light of my resume, most of which were very high-visibility causing me to receive more personal recognition than I deserved. At the same time, I found myself resenting how much time I was spending at work. I began to arrive closer and closer to starting time, and like the vast majority of people who work in large—and largely impersonal—corporations, I came to the point where I was ready to leave the moment the time clock displayed quitting time.

In fact, one of the most important lessons I learned while working at GM was where the most dangerous place in the world is located. (In reality, this place is not unique to GM and actually exists in many organizations in all kinds of industries.) When I share with people that I learned this lesson while working at GM, many people immediately imagine large, dangerous machinery. And although we had lots of large, dangerous machinery where it is truly amazing that more people are not injured, working around that machinery was not the most dangerous place in the world. The most dangerous place in the world would have been about three feet outside any of the exit doors at quitting time—nothing could have kept anyone standing there from being trampled by the stampede of people who were running at top speed to the parking lot, where they would jump in their cars, burn some rubber getting out of the parking lots, presumably getting back to living. I know that most had been dead all day—we had become really, really good at playing the traditional American work game called "How Little Can I Do Today and Not Get Fired?" That applies to both union and non-union workers alike. In fact, I learned the game from some of the best in the engineering department. In the "old days," our departmental secretary kept a calendar on her desk where we were supposed to check in and out of the engineering area when we went out into the million-plus-square-foot plant. Looking for a fellow engineer one day, I noticed that he had logged himself into a section of the plant with which I was unfamiliar—a place called IPH. Being a relative newcomer, that was not too surprising, so I quickly found one of the senior engineers to ask him how to find my engineer friend. Putting his index finger up to his lips in the universal signal for silence, he whispered, "That means 'in-plant holiday'—he didn't feel like working today, so he's out there walking around—lost in the plant. You'll never find him today!"

What's wrong with the game of "How Little Can I Do Today and Not Get Fired?" It took me some time to figure this out, but there is a real and diabolical consequence of this game. Consider this: If I am really good at this game, I will figure out a way to do a little less today than yesterday. In other words, my work would be worth less today than it was yesterday. If I am successful at putting together an entire career based on this philosophy, at the end of the career, I am likely to be doing so very little that I am, indeed, worthless—at least at my job. Therein lies the real problem with the game! How are you going to feel about yourself in general if the dominant activity of your life— the thing to which you devoted the most time for the longest period of time, your life's work—has left you feeling worthless? I have never found anyone whose attitudes and feelings about something they are doing for eight to ten hours a day do not affect how they feel about themselves and the rest of the hours they spend with family, friends, or community! It's a devastating personal reality. Here are some of the phrases people use to describe themselves in the midst of this type of working reality.

- *I feel trapped—I've got to work because I need the money, but I hate it!*

- *I have become really good at going "into my zone"—I don't really think about anything, and that's how I get through the day.*

- *Work is what I have to do—after work, it's MY time and I do what I want to do!*

So, if it's true that work will affect us—who we really are, how we feel about ourselves, and how we relate to others—a very important, though very personal question becomes, "Am I happy with the person I am becoming?" And very specifically, "Can I recognize the impact that my work is having on me and say it is helping me become the kind of person I most want to become?"

So, again we face the question, why are you working? Stated another way, what do you really want to get out of work? Here was my answer: I yearned for work that was fulfilling, work relationships that were satisfying, and a work experience that reinforced the values in the rest of my world.

How does that sound to you? Impossible dream? Idealistic?

Like me, you may wonder if this is possible. Let me share the "end" from the "beginning." It is possible! In a sense, the company that my partner and I formed has served as our laboratory for this grand experiment. One of the most exciting discoveries has been that the majority of the reason work does not feel like this in most places is actually not the fault of the place, but the result of the way we, as individuals, think about our work. That was certainly true for me. Let me be particularly clear about something from the outset—GM was, and is, a wonderful employer. The real problem was me and how I understood my work. I could be a much better employee at General Motors today as a consequence of this one, golden understanding. However, I needed the time "in the laboratory" to achieve the insights that make that true. The rest of this book is about the lessons we've learned, and applied, along the way. My passion is to help individuals reclaim the work time of their lives as a positive, healthy, life-giving experience, rather than the dull, stultifying, almost death-inducing place that so many experience today. Whether you love your work, hate your work, or are indifferent to it at this moment, I hope you'll consider adopting some of the principles in this book and applying them to your own work. This could be the most important, literally life-changing, and FUN thing you have ever done for yourself! ENJOY!!!

PART I:

---

*Creating a Culture
of Excellence*

CHAPTER 1:
A FRAMEWORK THAT WORKS

While working for General Motors, my future business partner and co-founder of our company, Ron Fauquher, and I were returning home late one night when I turned to him and said, "You know, Ron, if we are being flown all around the country to help other software engineers utilize mini- and microcomputers in their manufacturing operations, maybe we could do this on our own. Maybe this would be a pretty good idea for a business." His sagacious comment was, "We might think that's a good idea, but once we talk about leaving our current jobs and starting a company on our own, we're going to run into two very important obstacles—our wives!"

Undaunted, we both carried the idea home to our spouses. I had done this a few times before, and I actually knew Ron was right. While still in undergraduate school, I had thought that a Wendy's franchise looked like a great opportunity. My wife, Cindy, simply said, "Now, what do you know about making hamburgers?" When we began to have children and made the inevitable trips to the shoe store, I began to believe that selling children's shoes was a gold mine—at least, it seemed that way to me as a purchaser! She had the same sweetly spoken concern—"Honey, we don't know anything about selling shoes—we barely know enough to buy them!" So when I brought home the idea of starting a software company, her response blew me away. Very simply, she said, "That's a good idea.

You and Ron ought to pursue that one!" Amazingly, Ron talked his wife, Cheryl, into the same idea, and our new business was born.

Ron and I have always been planners. Uniquely for programmers, both of us have a fair amount of accounting in our backgrounds, so both of us enjoyed looking at the business opportunities in spreadsheet form. Like every good business plan, ours began with a mission statement, and the initial mission of our little company was something like: "We will be a software company driven by Christian principles and ethics that serves business, industry, and government." In other words, do anything software-related for anybody, and do it ethically—not exactly a textbook example of a mission statement, we can now readily admit!

We have always had an outside board of directors to guide and advise us, so when they challenged us to look closely at our business model and think about whether or not we should build the company around a consulting model, (billing for hours worked), or build the company around a product model, (billing for products delivered), we ran two sets of business plans. It seemed to us that the higher leverage for our business would undoubtedly be in the product model, but we also recognized that we needed to find a way to bridge the financial gap if we were going to stop billing long enough to build some products. This decision led us to seek a financial partner, and Ontario Corporation, a privately held, very successful manufacturing company headquartered in our community, agreed to help us fund the gap. Just to fill in the history very briefly, we ultimately became Ontario Systems Corporation while we were part of the Ontario family of companies, and operated that way until August of 2003, when Ontario Corporation agreed to sell the company back to the original management team.

During the mid-'80s, Ontario Corporation began a long-term strategic planning process, coordinated by a newly hired president of the corporation. Challenged to update our plans, which were to be reviewed directly by the new holding company president, our team put together what we believed was an A+ plan. We had a mission statement, goals, sub-goals, tactics, and it all crystallized in a forty-page, detailed operating budget for the next five years of operations. We submitted our masterpiece, and then we waited for our "grade."

Finally, almost two weeks later, the bound plan was returned from Corporate. I quickly searched every page for any comments or signs of approval. To my undying disappointment, there was absolutely no trace of affirmation to be found in the entire document! However, on page one, at the very top under the mission statement paragraph, the word, "Christian" had been circled in red, and out to the side were scrawled these words, "Whose are these?"

"Whose are these, indeed," I thought. "Isn't that like asking who is buried in Grant's tomb?" So, as I typically do when someone does something I don't understand, I picked up the phone and I engaged my relatively new "boss" in a dialogue. It went something like this.

"George," I asked, "I couldn't help but notice that you circled the word Christian in our mission statement, and you wrote a question in the margin about whose they were, so I wanted to ask, what exactly do you mean by that?"

"Well, Wil," he calmly replied, "what I meant was, are those your Christian principles, are they mine, are they Jim Bakker's, or Jimmie Swaggart's—just whose Christian principles and ethics are you referring to?" (You may recall that both Jims, Bakker and Swaggart, were having their issues back then.)

"Oh," I began rather sheepishly, because I could see where he was going, and I thought he had a good point, "what you're saying is that because we've said something so broad, it might not mean much at all, right?"

George replied, in a style very typical of my friends at Ontario Corporation, "well, you might want to consider that." And we hung up.

This left me with two primary thoughts. First, I did not want to consider removing the reference to a set of values and ethics which I thought were part of lending meaning to the workplace. This was during a period of time when many companies had adopted mission statements that were as simple, and impoverished (in my opinion) as, "enhance shareholder value." It was not an immoral goal in and of itself, but neither did it provide any direction, vision, or personal motivation for the entire stakeholder set of workers. We will discuss this concept further in a later chapter, but even this early in my experience of operating a business, I knew that removing values from the corporate cloth would leave it worthless for inspiring day-to-day commitment.

The second thought I had about my conversation with George was, "Hmm, I wonder what I do next?"

When I'm stuck, I often seek help in books. In this case, I began going through textbooks on business planning and strategic planning processes. As I flipped the pages of George Steiner's book, entitled *Strategic Planning*, I found this quote from Thomas Watson, Jr. on page 151:

> "This then is my thesis: I firmly believe that any business, in order to survive and achieve success must have a sound set of beliefs on which it premises all its policies and actions—

In other words, the basic philosophy, spirit, and drive of an organization have far more to do with its relative achievements than do technological or economic resources, organization structure, innovation and timing. All these things weigh heavily on success, but they are, I think, transcended by how strongly the people in the organization believe in these precepts and how faithfully they carry them out."

Exactly! That's what I actually believed, but had never seen or heard it expressed so well. And the fact that the person who said it was Thomas Watson, Jr., the leader who helped IBM so completely dominate the computer systems business during the '50s and '60s made my personal interest very intense. But, this didn't read like a typical mission statement. Where was I in this book?

I was in a chapter on "Developing Basic Business Purposes and Missions," in a section entitled "Company Creed or Philosophy Statements." Immediately, it occurred to me that most of us are probably trying to make our mission statements do more than they are meant to do. Bound by getting them down to one memorable sentence, we had resorted to overly broad words, which, as my friend had pointed out to me, ultimately weakened rather than strengthened the message.

Of course, this presented a new challenge. We had not articulated our corporate philosophy, and I began to wonder if it could be done adequately to serve the needs of all persons on a staff. However, once we took off the "straight jacket" of trying to fit an entire philosophy into a subset of a mission statement, I was amazed at how good it felt to pen a few paragraphs about life, work, and how they might work together. Gathering my thoughts carefully, indeed prayerfully, in this important assignment, I began to write.

Before I share the outcome, please understand that this is how I expressed our corporate philosophy. Thankfully, it has stood the test of time with hundreds of diverse employees. However, for this to provide the same level of satisfaction and fulfillment for you, I encourage you to write your own philosophy. You are free to borrow ideas and concepts you find helpful. You should feel equally free to add or delete concepts that will make the final document one that you and your team fully own. I know that the value for us has been in the explanation, not the written words. The value continues to be manifest as we strive to live up to our own best goals as represented by these words—both individually and corporately.

Finally, I would encourage you to distill your paragraphs into keywords or mnemonics that will provide a memorable, shorthand notation by which you can communicate and inculcate these concepts into the fabric of your organization. In our case, the paragraphs came first and the keywords came second. Your experience may be the opposite. The value is in finding a way that you can discuss this with your entire team. And then the value pays dividends as it guides policies and actions for your entire company.

I will devote a chapter of explanation to each of these paragraphs, but here is the framework that works from my perspective.

Statement of Corporate Philosophy

The basic philosophy that drives the organization of Ontario Systems is summarized in the following statements:

Stewardship

We believe that all of life is a gift from God. Our work at Ontario Systems is part of that gift.

Integrity

We believe that good stewardship of this gift is expected of each of us. Our work at Ontario Systems reflects our stewardship of this particular gift.

Service

We believe that the best example of a life of good stewardship is the life of Jesus Christ. It is His example we would follow in making daily decisions.

Tolerance

We believe that each person has responsibility for the stewardship of their own life. It is not the responsibility of Ontario Systems to assume that personal duty. It is our responsibility to encourage each other in thoughtful evaluation of the action that stewardship requires.

Professionalism

We believe these principles are the keys to work that is fulfilling, relationships that are satisfying, and a consistency of purpose that unites all of life.

CHAPTER 2:

STEWARDSHIP

"We believe that all of life is a gift from God.
Our work at Ontario Systems is part of that gift."

Without doubt, a statement of corporate philosophy with which one is comfortable—one that enhances our appreciation of work and life in general—will be a philosophy based on a foundation common to our statement of personal philosophy. I know of very few persons who have written their personal philosophy, but I think it fundamentally true that we all behave based on our own personal philosophies, regardless of how well they are articulated.

Therefore, the first paragraph of our corporate philosophy touches a bedrock of personal philosophy to which most persons find ready agreement. In the annals of human history, most people have believed in a God. It's relatively atypical to find individuals who claim they do not. We call such persons atheists, a word that literally means "no-God" or "without God." Although still a decided minority, there are many more persons who will claim to be unsure about God. After all, they reason, how can a finite being (like us) be sure of anything that has different dimensions and a scale beyond our finite ability to comprehend. We call these people "agnostics," a word that literally means "no knowing" or "without knowledge" specifically referring to God. Agnostics are, for the most part, willing to admit the possibility of a God, but simply claim to be unable to verify God's existence from a human perspective. Some may find the reference to God in this paragraph unnecessary, but for me, in a discussion far outside the scope of this book, it is both an honest and helpful reference point.

The basic idea of this paragraph is simply that life, and the work we do during our earthly lives, is a gift that we are unable to give ourselves. Contrary to the popular notion rolling around, particularly in Western culture today that people "earn" their stations in life, the best thinkers of human history have generally agreed that life has been spawned intentionally, and it has been God's intention that has been fulfilled rather than ours. In his landmark book on helping people find meaning and purpose in life, Rick Warren begins the book, *The Purpose Driven Life*, with the arresting statement, "It's not about you." His fundamental premise is simply this: Unless we can take credit for designing life, we can't figure out the purpose of life by asking ourselves. We must think about the Creator's purpose and find a way to ask Him or Her!

Therefore, if life is a gift, and our work a part of the gift, what is a reasonable response? In one word, I have come to believe it is stewardship.

Having already confessed that I am a P.K. (preacher's kid), I know the word *stewardship* can elicit some uncomfortable responses. Perhaps the word has become perverted by the way some churches euphemize asking for money to meet an institutional need for cash flow when they use the sacramental term, stewardship. However, true stewardship has much broader implications than how we spend our money. Money is one measure, but it's only one. From a philosophical perspective, I love the fuller meaning of stewardship. A steward is one who manages on behalf of the real owner. My favorite brief job description for steward is this: Do the most you can with whatever you've been given to do with!

How much time do we have? Did we use it well? What are the unique talents and abilities that define us? Are we using them to get the most of them? Did we use resources entrusted to us well, or have we squandered them? Being a good steward is a tough standard to live up to, but it's a great standard.

Businesses have many stakeholders: investors/owners, employees, customers, vendors, and even their communities. What should be the standard of conduct toward each of these interested parties? Very importantly, what should be the time frame by which that is measured? Short-term temptations to sacrifice the long-term betterment are rarely the right solution. While each circumstance will have its own merits, in general, a steward is always asking "What's the best, long-term strategy for the real owner?" A steward is constantly balancing the needs of the many stakeholders with the good of the business. A steward will routinely need to deal with questions like, "How can we balance the needs of employees with those of either investors or customers?" When I think of a business as "mine" rather than recognizing accountability to another owner, I may be tempted to make short-term, self-serving decisions rather than balancing the needs of all stakeholders over the long term. When we see all of life as a gift, our only reasonable response is to treat the gift with thoughtfulness and care. Ultimately, that will really please the Giver (whomever you understand that to be) and most likely provide consistent, thoughtful balance to the many stakeholders we truly serve.

The final benefit of treating the business as a gift, even if you had a hand in getting it started, is that it protects us from one of the most dangerous of moral failings—pride. Again, surveying across religions and philosophies, it seems that most thinking persons have come to the conclusion that at the center of all kinds of evil things is this issue of pride. Once you start a business, or begin to assume leadership positions in a business, there will be all kinds of people glad to help inflate your ego with well-meaning compliments and flattery.

It used to happen more often when the business was newer, but as Ron and I would find our way into various community activities, inevitably some well-meaning person would come up to us to congratulate us on starting a business. "You guys must be REALLY smart. You started a software business. It looks like it's quite a success. Things are looking really good for you guys. You must be REALLY smart."

All the while they were talking, I was thinking about what they were saying. My first thought was, "Isn't it amazing how deceptive appearances can be!" Remember, these were the early days—we were still wondering if it could be a commercial success ourselves! My second thought was, "I wonder if it's true that we're successful because we're smart—or because we work hard—or because of *fill in the blank*." I'd look at Ron, and I'd say to myself, "Well, he is smart, but frankly, he's not that smart!" And Ron would look at me and say to himself, "Well, being smart can't be the reason, cause sometimes he's just plain dumb!" Honestly, we had both known individuals who were much smarter than we were who had started businesses that had failed. Conversely, we knew people who, from a raw horsepower point of view, were probably not as "smart" as either of us, yet they had been incredibly successful in a commercial sense. Maybe it was because we had each other to help us avoid believing what others were saying, but from everything we could observe, the work itself and any incumbent commercial success was a gift. We were simply determined to make the most of whatever gift came to us, and to be very thankful for it!

CHAPTER 3:
INTEGRITY

"We believe that good stewardship of this gift is expected of each of us. Our work at Ontario Systems reflects our stewardship of this particular gift."

How does one measure good stewardship? How can we really know what others are capable of doing? This seems like an "inside" value—one that is only known to every individual from their own "inside."

I remember well bringing home my report cards to my parents. I knew on my "inside" that the fact that I did well in school was not because I worked hard at it, nor because I worked any harder at it than other friends who struggled. School was generally pretty easy for me. In today's vernacular, it must have fit my "learning style," it must have been appropriate to my cultural bias, or some other sociologically correct reason for achievement. Nevertheless, on report card day, it was tempting beyond reason to seek affirmation for getting good grades. Invariably, when I came through the door at home, my mother would greet us, and I was always anxious to see how she reacted. Quickly, I would thrust the card into her hands and ask, "What do you think, Mom?" And after only a brief glance at the report card, she looked at me directly in the eyes and asked, "Did you do your best this grading period?"

"Mom, I got all A's!" I protested.

"I'm really glad that your report card is very strong, but it's more important to always do your best. Someday, you may not get all A's, and when that happens, it will really be important to answer that question, 'Did you do your best?' Because our best is the real measure of how well we're doing. We can't do better than that, but only we know when we've actually done it!"

Somebody may be thinking, "Man, did she YUK your WOW!!!" True, but I think my "WOW" was so secondary to the real lesson she was trying to teach me that I think it's totally OK. In other words, when you try to take credit for things you don't deserve, you deserve to get YUKed! My mom is one wise woman!

So, the measure of stewardship is taken by our personal integrity. I love the etymology of words and the particularly rich meanings one can derive by understanding a word's origins. For example, the word *integrity* in its root form has nothing to do with dishonesty or truth-telling. It comes from the same root word as the words "integer" and "integrated." It refers to wholeness, completeness, or entirely together. When we use the word today, what it really means is that the thing we are observing has complete consistency. It has to do with the whole issue of personal integration—do our words match our deeds—do our attitudes accurately reflect our beliefs—are we whole?

One of the major dangers of compartmentalizing our work world from the rest of our lives is the danger of losing our personal integrity—of literally disintegrating (falling apart) due to the stresses of work values and societal mores that are contradictory to how we would truly like to live.

I learned that stress firsthand early in my career when I was asked to accompany my direct supervisor to a meeting with our plant's general manager to help cost justify a factory automation project on which I was to be the lead programmer. The meeting seemed to be somewhat spontaneous, because we had never discussed cost justification before, so our only preparation was what we could discuss in the halls on the way to the general manager's office. I began the conversation by saying, "You know, I'm not sure we can actually cost justify this project based on savings. We may have less direct labor costs, but it will not be insignificant to keep this line running due to the severe environment in which the technology will be running. I suspect that if we simply managed our people better in the existing, more manual system, we would probably do even better than we will be able to do with automation."

My boss never broke stride. He kept walking resolutely toward the Big Boss's office and said to me with only a faint grin on his face, "That's OK, Wil. Just tell yourself a lie long enough and you'll start to believe it!"

I was dumbfounded! What was I going to say to the Big Boss? Have you ever been there, knowing that someone you respect and in authority expects you to lie to achieve their goals? It's VERY uncomfortable. Fortunately for me, the general manager was not in his office that afternoon. I never had to say anything at all about that project. But I never forgot how it felt to be in that bind.

By the way, what's wrong with the statement, "Just tell yourself a lie long enough and you'll start to believe it?" There's just one thing: It's true! We can erode our personal integrity one little tiny lie at a time, and each lie does, in fact, become easier to believe.

(For those who want to read about the groundbreaking research in this area, please see the work of Dr. Leon Festinger on the subject he called "cognitive dissonance." There are innumerable applications of his research in business and in life—very important, but beyond what we will discuss here.)

Let me add a personal speculation about integrity. I have come to believe that personal integrity may, in fact, be a sacred value. It seems to me that integrity is the value that allows us to stay in relationship with each other. From what I have been able to observe and research, most religions teach that people are actually eternal creations. We live for a few decades in this dimension, and then the real us "ejects" from the earth-suit that we wear while on the surface of the earth, continuing to live thereafter in another dimension beyond our earthbound ability to actually see or touch. However, personalities and relationships are considered more durable than earth-suits, and most who have written or taught about what happens after earthly death believe those things go on. If that's so—and that's for individuals to decide for themselves, I'm just reporting what most have concluded on the subject— then integrity takes on this additional dimension that I've called sacred.

Is integrity necessary for relationships? I find that I can actually stay in relationship with people who are honest. Some people like us, agree with us, and want to be of help. Some people don't like us, don't agree with us, and don't want to be of help. In either of those circumstances, when people are honest, we can stay in relationship because we know what to expect of the other person. However, in circumstances where someone claims to like us, agree with us, and want to help us, but actually behaves as though they don't want to do any of the three, it's a very different story. Those people are actually treacherous, saying one thing to your face while sticking a knife in your back. I do not know how to be in relationship with people who are dishonest. So, I conclude that integrity is a prerequisite for relationship. And if relationships can go on forever, integrity may be a sacred value.

I have come to believe that one should not aspire to higher virtues until one has first determined to have personal integrity. It's a foundational value that measures the quality of our stewardship and allows us to be in relationship with others. When we are building communities—whether it's a family unit, a city, or even a business—integrity is a core value.

CHAPTER 4:
SERVICE

"We believe that the best example of a life of good stewardship is the life of Jesus Christ. It is His example we would follow in making daily decisions."

There is a problem with choosing values like stewardship and integrity as the foundation stones on which you would like to build your corporate culture. The problem is that they are such internal values that it can be difficult to know what that means to the community. Everyone seems to agree that those are great values, but most want to know in a more operational sense what they mean. If you asked me to define them more specifically for any individual, I would admit that I am unable to do so. However, we might try to pick a good example of someone who was an outstanding steward with perfect integrity to see if we could pick up a clue about how to live this out with each other. The third paragraph does just that.

I realize that there are those who will object to me picking an example of someone who is better known as a great religious teacher than a business leader. However, due to my personal background, this is someone I've studied quite a bit over the years, and what I'd like to do is offer him as an example of the consummate "organization guy."

Regardless of what individuals have done with Jesus as a religious figure—an important, but very personal decision, which I respect and will not address in this book—I think it can be persuasively argued that Jesus is a corporate leader worth understanding. Consider this, from a businessperson's perspective:

- He spent only three years in executive management.

- He hired only twelve vice presidents—one of whom did not work out well by our standards.

- His organization has lasted over 2,000 years.

- His organization functions worldwide. Where it is healthy, it is making the world a better place. I'm the first one to admit it's not healthy in every location, but after studying what he actually taught, I've become persuaded that the unhealthiness is due to the way we've perverted what he taught, not what he actually said.

So, when I compare his success to my wildest aspirations, I have to admit that he has done something I have not even dared to dream for our organization. A reasonable question from which we might benefit would be, "How did he do that? What was his secret?"

There is a wonderful story that records a dialogue he had with two of his strongest vice presidents about halfway through his tenure. The two were brothers, and they had apparently been talking about where the new organization was headed. In "business-speak," they approached Jesus together and, with my business guy's hat on, I think the conversation went something like this. (My apologies in advance to biblical literalists.)

James and John speaking to Jesus: "Wow! We're starting to get the big picture, Jesus. I know this probably sounds a little brash, but since we 'get it' and we're willing to do whatever it takes to be the best that we can be, would you make us the first two senior vice presidents when the time comes?"

Jesus, shaking his head, but with a twinkle in his eye, to James and John: "So, you two want to be known as the very best of them all, eh?" (You didn't know Jesus spoke Canadian?) "OK, here's what you need to do. If you will figure out how to be a servant to everyone you meet, you will, indeed, be the greatest of all!"

James and John to Jesus: "Thanks, man! You're the BEST!"

James and John to each other as they are leaving: "We got it! All we have to do is serve other people—HEY, wait a minute. What does that mean? I thought. . ."

I take from this wonderful story that the key to being a good steward with integrity is to be of service to other people. By the way, it's one thing to apply a standard to other people, especially one like service where you might actually end up being served better yourself. It's another matter entirely to apply that same standard to oneself. Just a little later in the story, Jesus is quoted as saying, "I didn't come to be served. I came to serve." Here is a guy who was literally "bigger than the Beatles" in his day; who could have commanded any number of people to do his absolute bidding at any time, and they would have done it gladly; and who in a reflective moment discloses that he is most fulfilled and most in line with his own sense of purpose when he is serving others. Could it be that we are all really wired that way?

Why do you suppose service is such a powerful organization builder? Think about this question: Who receives the most profound satisfaction from an act of service, the person receiving the service or the person giving the service? If we are ever in need of an antidote to feelings of worthlessness at work, we are probably measuring our value in the wrong way. Perhaps we have been measuring our worth by how many people serve us rather than by how many people we serve! One way of measurement will always leave us wanting more. One way will always leave us knowing our value.

There are four areas where we encourage our team members to seek fulfillment in serving others through their work: fellow employees, customers, vendors, and community. Let me start our thinking in each of these dimensions.

Serving fellow employees: One of the most fertile grounds in which to start finding fulfillment at work is in serving our fellow employees. When we think of an employee group as a team, it is easy to see how every member plays a part and serves each other. We don't need every team member to play the same position, but we do need every team member playing their own position, and playing it well! The first time that our staff is introduced to these values is during new employee orientation, so it is natural for many of our newer staff members to feel as though there are not a lot of ways to serve the more senior employees on the team. However, even in this circumstance, I remind them that simply being there is a huge encouragement to the team. We need the help, and we are excited to see new talent added to the pool. In this circumstance, service may simply look like being a really good student—learning quickly, asking great questions, being attentive. At the very least, within a short time, there will be another group of new hires who will be looking for someone to help them find the restrooms, learn where to go for lunch, find out the best person to ask in various circumstances, etc. The opportunities for service to our team are all around us—all we need to do is look.

Serving Customers: Although customers generally pay us to serve them, that fact alone can make it difficult to make customers feel as though they have been uniquely well-served! "After all," they might reason, "I expected you to serve me, and I deserve it since I've paid for it." That's true, and since we have all been customers, we can probably identify with that sentiment. So, how do we go about leaving a customer feeling really well-served? I have come to believe that there are two things we must do to make customers feel well-served: 1) We must set their expectations accurately, and 2) then we must exceed those expectations with the delivered service.

1. Setting expectations has two components. First, we must tell the customer what we will do, and then we must tell the customer what we won't do. Most of us find it easy to talk about what we will do. We want to please the customer; they explain their problem, and we think we understand it and agree to fix it. In my experience, however, if we don't go to the second step of telling them what the limits are on our service, the customer will be left with the impression that we will do anything and everything to solve their problems—normally at a fixed price, by the way. Their expectations have no limits, and almost without fail, any "surprise" will come as a negative surprise thereafter. One of my associates is fond of saying that "If you can't tell them what you won't do as well as what you will do, you probably just don't understand what they want you to do in the first place!" From experience, that's wise advice!

2. There are also two ways in which we can exceed customer
    expectations. Now that we have been careful to set their
    expectations, we can simply and literally do more than
    we said we would do. In the software business, these
    opportunities abound. If there is a request for a custom
    piece of software, exceed the specification document. (Is
    it obvious you can't exceed the specification document
    unless there is one? Yet so many software companies
    rely on inadequate definition documents—including us
    from time to time! OK, I'm off the soapbox. . . apply
    this to your business.) This is a fairly straightforward
    way in which to exceed customer expectations. The
    only additional advice I would offer is to be sure to tell
    the customer specifically that you've exceeded their
    agreed-upon expectations. Many times, the "extra" that
    we do is below the radar screen and would otherwise be
    unnoticed and unappreciated. It is fair and right to let
    them know of your diligent and conscientious service—
    otherwise, they may legitimately not realize what you
    have done for them.

    The second way to exceed customer expectations is one
    that I would not have guessed when I first got started in
    business. The second way is this: Be the nicest customer
    service organization with whom your customer deals.
    They will both appreciate and pay for your competent
    courtesy. This point was driven home for me several
    years ago when we made the decision to integrate a
    popular word processing package into our software.
    When we did so, we realized that we could not charge a
    traditional recurring maintenance fee for support of this
    integrated product because its manufacturer provided
    toll-free phone lines and free application support to all
    of its licensees. Since you can't charge less than zero,

we decided that we would not provide contract support, but that if one of our customers would like to have us help them with their word processing issues, we would charge them at our standard hourly support rate, which was $120 per hour at the time. Much to our surprise, our customers routinely called our help lines for word processing support! When we asked them why they would call us when the service was free from the manufacturer, they told us how great our support staff was, how helpful they were because they understood the application, and how very "nice" they were. By being competent and courteous, customers "felt" served. This was a wonderful revelation to all of us! Nice guys can finish first!

Service to Vendors: In my mind, this is one of the most under-taught concepts in business schools today. At the risk of stating the obvious, vendors are the people we pay to serve us. We are their customers. So, they have all the same issues with making us feel well-served that I just outlined in the discussion on serving customers. However, I believe serving vendors is good business, and I know it's a way to derive satisfaction from your work. Very simply, be aware of opportunities to serve vendors and you will enjoy it! In today's technologically interrelated world, no vendor is any better than the complex of vendors who are working together to provide a solution. Nurturing those relationships is both pragmatic and fun. I encourage people to get creative with this whole concept.

What might this look like? It looks like expressions of appreciation for good service. It means saying "thanks" to a service technician who is working on (even if they have not yet solved) a problem. It means treating them the way we would like our customers to treat us. It means paying bills on time, within terms. It means communicating directly and professionally when we cannot.

For a slightly more creative example of what this might look like, let me explain a bit about our business and an opportunity we had to serve a vendor in a unique way. We sell proprietary software that depends on other manufacturers' hardware and software. Several years ago, our database vendor released a new version of their database to the field and we sent it to several of our clients to bring their systems up to date. Unfortunately, once our customers began to load the new version, a devastating error was discovered that caused the entire system to become unstable upon certain circumstances—circumstances that were inevitable, but not predictable as to when they would occur. We notified our vendor/partner and told them of the crisis. We tried to keep the bombs from detonating in the field in order to buy time to get a fix from our vendor that would prevent the problem. After working around the clock for two days, they delivered an ad hoc release—and it worked! We deployed the ad hoc to our customers, averted several data disasters, and began to celebrate. I was very pleased with the way our staff responded, liberally passing e-mail and phone call compliments to our database vendor's staff. I had been personally involved in escalating the crisis, and I judged this to be a truly extraordinary event with a heroic response. So, I placed a call to a friend on the "inside" of our vendor's company and asked her to help me throw a surprise "thank-you party" for their staff. It was nothing fancy—just punch and cookies on a Friday afternoon to express appreciation for the outstanding response we had received to a potentially disastrous circumstance. Our vendor was incredulous that we would treat them with appreciation for a problem they actually caused! Even today, we are not their largest customer, but if one were to ask them which of their customers they would prefer to work with, they will answer, Ontario Systems.

Why do we work at providing extraordinary service, even to vendors? Yes, there can be a business "payback" when the vendor recognizes the extraordinary customer who is serving them. But, the real reason is much more personal. Remember the secret of service! The person who provides the service always gets more joy than the person receiving it. Although we sent them an entire party, it is probably mostly forgotten by them these several years later; but, I'm still telling this story! Apply the secret of service at every dimension. Put it to the test. I'm confident you'll agree with the biblical observation that it is "more blessed to give than to receive."

Service to Community: One of the concepts in which we believe deeply is the concept of being positively and proactively involved in the communities in which we operate. We encourage our people to be involved in making the communities where they live better places. If we all "bloom where we are planted," the world will become a better place in more ways than we can imagine. Since we do not sell our products in a local market, there is no direct commercial benefit in the short-term to such involvement. We encourage this involvement and activity on the basis of constantly improving the quality of life for everyone within our various communities, and on the principle of service. We know that these are very satisfying and fulfilling ways to extend oneself.

In many dimensions, the people who work at our company are among the most fortunate. They are both employed in an economy where many are not, and they are fully employed. We can almost guarantee that we will utilize all the talents and abilities our staff can bring as we serve a fast-paced, technologically challenging market. Like our ideas about stewardship, serving our communities just seems like a good way to show appreciation for the gifts we have been uniquely given in our work. We believe that we are blessed in order to be a blessing, and community service is just one more way to express that in action.

I'm not sure why it took me so long to understand this principle of service. Once I understood it, I remembered an experience from my childhood and a lesson taught to me by my older brother, Richard. Rich was an awesome older brother. Since he was eight years older, he was, in my mind, the perfect age to teach me about all the important things: cars, sports, and most importantly, girls. So that you can more fully appreciate his virtue in this respect, I suppose I should tell you that I have a twin brother, too. In other words, for each of these "life lesson" type of events which he turned into teachable moments, he had not one, but two, snot-nosed little brothers to think about. We thought it was a great idea for him to take us to the school to play basketball with the "big boys" every time he went—and often, he did. We thought it was an even better idea to let us go with him on a car date—and never once did he allow that! Always wise beyond his years, my twin brother and I realize that we were blessed by his love for us.

In reality, even my twin and I would admit that eight years of age difference could get on one's nerves! It was one of those nerve-wracking moments where Rich tried to teach me the secret of the service principle, although I failed to apply it in the workplace for many years. About halfway through the traditional summer vacation from school, I remember coming into a room where he was reading. It was probably a really lame way to try to engage my older brother in some summertime activity, but upon seeing him in the room, I began to whine, "I'm bored. I've got nothing to do." Sizing up the situation in about a nanosecond, Rich said flatly, "You know what your problem is? You're only thinking about yourself. If you'll think of something to do for someone else you won't be bored and you won't have 'nothing' to do!"

I always hated it when he was right! But he was right!

You know, we haven't changed the name of "work" to "play." You'll not hear us talking about, "Hey, let's get up and go to play today." We still get up and go to work! The truth is that there are days where it requires some discipline to get up and go to a productive day at the office. How do you get yourself up? What's the self-talk that helps you pull yourself up by the bootstraps and go make a difference? How about this: "I'm going to work today. I have fellow employees who need me to help them. I have customers who are counting on me. I have vendors who are working on my issues today and they need my help to finish the work." In other words, who will I serve today? Understanding the golden key of service is the shortest path I know to finding true fulfillment in our work.

Chapter Footnote: I realize that I am not unique in suggesting that Jesus is an excellent model for leadership. My upbringing helped me to reach that conclusion independently, but I have been pleased as an adult to find many other compelling books on the subject. Among the most forthright books/authors on this topic would be: *Jesus, CEO*, by Laurie Beth Jones; *Roaring Lambs*, by Bob Briner; and almost anything by John Maxwell. For any who would enjoy exploring that topic specifically, I can recommend any and all of these resources.

CHAPTER 5:

TOLERANCE—RESPECT FOR THE INDIVIDUAL

"We believe that all persons have responsibility for the stewardship of their own lives. It is not the responsibility of Ontario Systems to assume that personal duty. It is our responsibility to encourage each other in the thoughtful evaluation of the action that stewardship requires."

Hovering over the booth assembly that we were erecting at a trade show, one of my associates and I had been talking about corporate philosophies and other things philosophical when he stopped what he was doing, looked over at me, and said in his own, inimitable way, "Honest people disagree." After thinking about that profound little statement for a while, I could see the truth of it. Only dishonest people could possibly agree all the time. Sometimes, honest people come to different conclusions.

The best evidence I can offer for the truth of this statement is my wife. Although we've been married for more than thirty years now, she still has not concluded that I am, in fact, always right! I married my high school sweetheart after our freshman year of college. I've known her since we were sixteen. She is the kind of person who could not tell a convincing lie if her life depended on it. In spite of my best efforts to the contrary, however, she does not always agree with me!

That's a fact—now what do we do? The same fact will hold true for people with whom we work. What is the glue that will hold us together when we are seeing the same circumstance through different lenses? In the corporate setting, what are the limits of personal responsibility and group accountability?

Fundamentally, I don't believe healthy people set out to waste their lives. When we see that self-destructive type of behavior, in most circumstances we can readily identify it as a sickness. Setting that observation in place as a foundational premise, it is easy for me to allow the pendulum to swing toward personal responsibility for individual behavior. It's not the company's responsibility to steward an individual's life. It is fully that person's responsibility. Does that mean there is no accountability to the company? No, the company, and specifically, ALL the people who make up the company, have the responsibility (not privilege) to encourage each other as to what action good stewardship might demand in a given situation. In effect, we are holding people accountable to their own understanding of good stewardship. Since our belief and experience match in this area—that is, people truly want to do what's best if they know what that might be—this method of mutual accountability works really well.

We have given this paragraph the one-word mnemonic of tolerance. Because the word *tolerance* is sometimes misunderstood in our culture, we have added the words, "Respect for the Individual" so that people won't become distracted by a particular word and ignore the importance of the concept. The word *tolerance* is occasionally maligned today by people who seem to use it to mean agreement. Tolerance does not mean agreement. In fact, it means that we can get along in spite of the fact that we don't necessarily agree. In my experience, tolerance, or respect, is a virtue that we expect people to extend to us automatically, yet it is a virtue we are reluctant to give to others.

Over the years I have been explaining the concept, I have never found a better way to talk about it than by sharing the famous poem by John Godfrey Saxe called "The Blind Men and the Elephant."

The Blind Men and the Elephant
Author: John Godfrey Saxe

It was six men of Indostan,
    To learning much inclined,
Who went to see the Elephant
    (Though all of them were blind),
That each by observation
    Might satisfy his mind.

The *First,* approached the Elephant,
    And happening to fall
Against his broad and sturdy side,
    At once began to bawl:
"God bless me! But the Elephant
    Is very like a wall!"

The *Second,* feeling of the tusk,
    Cried: "Ho! What have we here
So very round and smooth and sharp?
    To me 'tis mighty clear
This wonder of an Elephant
    Is very like a spear!"

The *Third* approached the animal,
    And, happening to take
The squirming trunk within his hands,
    Thus boldly up and spake:
"I see," quoth he, "the Elephant
    Is very like a snake!"

The ***Fourth*** reached out his eager hand,
　　And felt about the knee:
"What most this wondrous beast is like
　　Is mighty plain," quoth he:
"'Tis clear enough the Elephant
　　Is very like a tree!"

The ***Fifth***, who chanced to touch the ear,
　　Said: "E'en the blindest man
Can tell what this resembles most:
　　Deny the fact who can,
This marvel of an Elephant
　　Is very like a fan!"

The ***Sixth*** no sooner had begun
　　About the beast to grope,
Than, seizing on the swinging tail
　　That fell within his scope,
"I see," quoth he, "the Elephant
　　Is very like a rope!"

And so these men of Indostan
　　Disputed loud and long,
Each in his own opinion
　　Exceeding stiff and strong.
Though each was partly in the right
　　And all were in the wrong!

What a wonderful metaphor for all of us! Aren't we all relatively blind people who have simply touched different parts of this elephantine reality that we call life? Imagine a day in which we're riding on top of the elephant, we're guiding him around exactly where we want to go, completely in charge, and we see someone in the hall to whom we give an enthusiastic, "Good morning!" The person whom we have just greeted with utmost enthusiasm, warm smile, and genuine good wishes returns our well-intended greeting with a grunt.

What happened? "Oh, that's just her. She's always like that." "You know him—he's always a bear in the morning!" Maybe we just write them off completely—quit giving them our spectacular greetings if that's how they're going to react.

Are any of those responses helpful? They might be consistent with human nature, but we aren't helping anything by labeling or withdrawing. What would be helpful? We could simply ask ourselves, "I wonder what part of the elephant they've been touching?" You know, it could be that the elephant has just trampled over them! Maybe they've been gored by the elephant! Maybe they have been standing way too close to the tail of the elephant—not a good place to be! But doesn't life trample us, gore us, even poop on us sometimes? Maybe that person in the hallway is dealing with an addictive teenager. Maybe last night, her husband walked out. Maybe this week the news at the doctor's office was not good. Life from their view of the elephant looks really different.

How do we get along with people who are honest and disagree with us? If we could just recognize how limited our view of the world really is, and how unlikely it is to be just like the person's view with whom we are dealing, that would be a great place to start.

You've probably heard the saying, "Seek first to understand, more than to be understood" (from the Prayer of St. Francis of Assisi). I know my wife wishes I would get this one right. My tendency is to think about how to better explain my point of view the entire time she is explaining hers. She's touching a different part of the elephant, and I need to listen carefully to enlarge my own view of the situation. There may be an elephant-like picture emerging that will help both of us understand each other, and even life, more fully.

At the end of day, one of the things I want most from my life, including my work life, is to look back and realize that I now see more of the elephant than I did at the beginning. I hope that's one of your goals, too!

CHAPTER 6:

PROFESSIONALISM

"We believe these principles are the keys to work that is fulfilling, relationships that are satisfying, and a consistency of purpose that unites all of life."

What would it be like if we, and everyone in our organization, were able to consistently be a good steward with perfect integrity by serving our fellow employees, customers, vendors, and community while having utmost respect for individuals in the process? How would the rest of the world perceive such a person or organization?

A few years ago, we went through an exercise to understand and promote our corporate brand. We were contemplating a logo change, but that brought with it the opportunity to assess ourselves within our customer base and our chosen markets, as the logo is just one component of a corporate brand. Within this assessment was an interesting question which was asked of our customers: If Ontario Systems was a person, who are they? With a uniformity of answer that surprised even our expert facilitators, the most common answer to the question was, "They would be Michael Jordan." When our facilitators drilled down on this answer in follow-up questioning, our customers said something like this,

"They're like Michael Jordan because they are very expensive, but they are also the very best. They are true professionals!"

What a wonderful assessment! What a spectacular compliment! As I thought about it, I realized that in order for that assessment to be true, every individual on the team with whom our customers had contact had managed to live up to a value system that I think is very hard for individuals, let alone an entire company. That corporate integrity had been labeled by our customers as professional!

Literally, the word professional means "to speak before" (pro=before + fess=speak). Consequently, a professor is "one who speaks before." I like to think that a true professional is, therefore, someone whose work speaks before them.

We do not make it a practice to share our Statement of Corporate Philosophy with prospects, wearing it on our sleeves saying, "Wouldn't you like to do business with a company with this type of corporate values?" These are internally promoted, but externally, our belief is that we are far better off trying to live the values rather than talk about them. Walk the talk. Everybody. All the time. Professionals!

Of course, some would say it is not prudent to publish your values, because it may look hypocritical if you fail to achieve them. I have two responses to that objection. First, we realize that we are not perfect people, and that we will not live up to these ideals perfectly. But we do want to be held accountable to them. We believe in them so strongly that it is painful to realize we have not achieved them consistently, and we believe work will be more fulfilling and relationships more satisfying if we can get back on track. So please, help us by holding us accountable to what we truly desire to become. That's a good thing. Second, I would opine that it is generally better to aim for a high target and miss than to aim for a low target and succeed. We are not perfect, but in striving for perfection, we get better. We do not always hit the target, but we believe the target is a worthy one, and we will not lower our goal to accommodate variations that achieve lesser results.

How do you want to be known? Will people call you a "true professional," or will they realize that you were only filling a spot at work? How do people know your organization? Would they say you are Michael Jordan? Wouldn't you want them to?

Creating a culture of excellence at work begins with establishing a place for people where they can become everything they were created to become. That's a very exciting challenge for us—a quest that generates extraordinary performance from the individuals, and ultimately, from the team. Adopting this type of corporate philosophy, creating the culture of your company on this type of foundation, is the minimum bid to play in the game of building high-performing organizations. Create the right culture, and the extraordinary performance is a by-product.

One final word about vocation: Vocation *is* the final word. This word comes from the same root word as the word vocal (Latin, *vocare*), which literally means "to call." In the best sense of the word, our vocation is our calling. It's the thing for which we are uniquely and specifically created to be able to do. When we are doing it, we are aware of an internal contentment that defies understanding. When we are not doing it, we are restless. As we've already discussed, I believe that each of us finds deep satisfaction—a true vocation—in understanding our work to be of service to someone else. When we build our lives, both work and non-work, on this principle, we do indeed find a "unity of purpose that unites all of life." What a place to be!

Discussion and Reflection Questions

1) What are the primary values in your company? How are they working for you, personally?

2) What values would you like to see added? Subtracted?

3) What one thing would make work more fulfilling for you? What or how can you begin to make that change real for you and your company?

PART II:

Leadership within
a Culture of Excellence

CHAPTER 7:
HIGH-PERFORMANCE LEADERSHIP

The renowned industrial engineer, W. Edwards Demming, was called to consult with a company that was facing declining market share, aggressive competition, and an often fractious and contentious leadership team, to help them determine the best steps to take in turning the company around. Demming called a meeting of the leadership team and asked them to tell him, in their own words, what they believed was the root cause of their problems. After much discussion, the group agreed that all problems ultimately ran uphill to the problem of too many people who were no longer fully engaged in the company and its mission. In their words, "There's just too much deadwood in this company!"

Demming reportedly came up with what I think is a classic response when he fired back at them, "Were they dead when you hired them, or have you killed them?"

Are there any unhealthy symptoms in our organizations? Some are obvious: high turnover, high absenteeism, low productivity. Some are more subtle: lack of innovation, down-line veto, walls between work groups. Even if we can identify the symptoms, we are left with Demming's insightful question: Were they like that when we hired them, or is there something about the way our organization functions that has squashed the vitality out of the workplace?

In Part I, we discussed the values that individuals can embrace in order to promote and sustain an environment where they can "be all that they can be." In this section, we are going to look at the unique and important role that leadership plays in making sure that those values are homogenously blended throughout the organization.

What exactly is leadership? While there are many definitions, my current favorite comes from none other than management guru, Stephen Covey, who defines leadership as "helping others to see their potential so clearly that they are inspired to achieve it."

I love that definition for two reasons. First, from where does it imply that the motivation to achieve comes: external or internal? Obviously, Covey believes that people are internally motivated to achieve if we can help them catch a glimpse of what their achievements might be. Second, I love the word "inspired" in the definition. Literally, the word means "to breathe into." What Covey's definition says is this: If we can help people see their potential, it has the effect of "breathing into" them the motivation to achieve it.

For far too many workers, work has done anything but breathe life into them! In fact, for many, work actually feels more like it is sucking the life out of them—they can't wait to leave work. The ultimate goal is to retire from work—this applies equally to workers at all levels in the organization. But as we discussed previously, I don't believe work was intended to have this dire consequence on humans. Further, I have come to believe that for those who are tasked with leadership responsibilities in organizations, a reasonable test of our effectiveness is whether or not we are "inspiring" our teams, breathing life into them, or "aspirating" our teams, sucking the life out of them.

How important is good leadership to an organization? A friend of mine, Kent Humphreys, who used to run a large distribution company and now is an author, lecturer, and volunteer leader of a large business trade association, came up with this quote which speaks to the importance of leadership. He says, "No matter how important you think leadership is, it's more important than you think it is." Kent is generally speaking to groups of business leaders, so he begins with the thought that they understand the importance of their role. But, he completes the thought by telling them that they have probably underestimated the true importance, the full weight, of their leadership responsibilities.

How aware are you of this foundational truth? Here is a simple test whereby we can test Kent's thesis. How many organizations can you name that achieved great things that did not have great leadership? I've been presenting that question to groups across the country for a few years now, and no one to date has come up with an example. Conversely, we can all think of organizations that seem to have everything going for them except leadership, and they are languishing in every metric by which one might traditionally measure organizational effectiveness. The image I have of leaderless organizations is the image of an amoeba. They swim meaninglessly on the Petri dish of life, an occasional sector seeming to pull in one direction only to be pulled back to center by an offsetting ooze on the opposite side of the organism. They are non-directional, and organizations without leadership will often push and pull against themselves, making no real forward progress, just like the amoeba.

Frankly, most people can be convinced of how important leadership is without much effort, and that can be somewhat intoxicating to our human egos. Soon, we are feeling somewhat self-inspired, and we can hear ourselves saying down deep inside, "Give me the ball and let me run. I'll show them leadership, and everyone will get in line!" It may not be quite that obvious, but with the health and future of our companies on the line, if we come to believe that we are surrounded by people who seem to enjoy their amoeba-like existence, it is a little tempting to feel that way, isn't it?

Let me share just one caveat about jumping to the front of the leadership line. From the wisdom literature of the New Testament, there is a troubling, little verse that says, "Not many of you should presume to be teachers (the moral leaders of James' day) because you know that we who teach (lead) will be judged more strictly." (James 3:1)

At one level, I confess, that just seems unfair. "You mean to tell me that if I am willing to get in there and provide some leadership so that we get something done and move this organization forward, that I get judged by a higher standard?" Of course, it's not me saying that, but that does seem to be what James is saying. And over the years of studying his writings, I have found it generally to be a poor practice to try to argue with James!

On another level, of course, we all know the truth of that statement. "So, if we're all on a bus together and the bus goes over a cliff, did the driver have more responsibility?" We all know the answer to this rhetorical question. Naturally, the driver has more responsibility. It's why I share this caveat regarding leadership. Leadership is a wonderful privilege, but it is also an awesome responsibility. Not many, as James says, should presume toward leadership. It's a BIG deal!

How can I know if I'm really "right" for leadership? There is no single answer to that question. I fully respect that leadership is not limited to organizational positions, that all of us provide levels of leadership at various times, and that each person's "calling" into vocational leadership is undoubtedly unique. I will give just one litmus test for anyone who aspires to leadership. I have known many people over the years whose motivation for becoming a leader has been to make old "so-and-so" toe the line. In essence, they are saying, "If I could be king/queen for a day, I'd force those people to change their attitudes, work habits, etc." The truth is, whether providing leadership in business, in our families (spouse and children), in social organizations, or wherever, the only person we can change is ourselves. If others are to change, they must choose to change themselves. Permanent, long-term change cannot be coerced or forced, it must be chosen. Remember, we have to help them "see their potential so clearly that they are inspired to achieve it" on their own! If, as a leader, we're not ready to change the way we work with other people by changing ourselves, then we may not be truly called into long-term leadership.

We've established what leadership is, how important it is, and even discussed the burden of leadership. So, what do leaders do?

Truthfully, there are more books on leadership than any one person can read or remember. Jim Collins's landmark book, *Good to Great*, has some of the most interesting empirical research on effective leadership that I have personally read. Pick it up to learn about "Level 5 Leaders" and what makes them effective. Almost anything by Max DuPree will be inspirational and encouraging as you learn from this incredible leader who led Herman Miller Corp. through their formative years and explosive growth. His leadership classic is titled, *Leadership Is an Art*. Most of Stephen Covey's works address leadership in some form, but he dedicated an entire tome to *Principle Centered Leadership*, and it is a worthy read. I consider John Maxwell an expert on leadership, and among his many books are two specifically related to leadership. The first, which became an almost instant classic in the literature was called *The 21 Irrefutable Laws of Leadership*, which he followed with a more personal view of leadership in a book called *The 21 Indispensable Qualities of a Leader*.

I've read these books, and I agree with all they teach—insofar as I can remember. And therein lies the only problem with them. If I were trying to follow just Maxwell, I'd have to remember forty-two things in order to be effective in leadership!

Personally, I needed a shorthand way to think about it. So, I've boiled it all down to only two major responsibilities for leaders. If we can do these two things well, we will probably be incredibly effective leaders. What are they?

1) Vision—Cast a compelling vision for what the organization is doing and why it is important.

2) Values—Articulate the values by which the organization will accomplish its vision.

These are the "spring training" fundamentals of providing leadership. Have you ever noticed what baseball teams do in spring training? They work on the basics. They don't practice a triple steal on a fake bunt. They practice fielding ground balls and catching pop flies. Once they get the basics, they can build on them, but it all starts with the basics. For those of us in leadership, getting these two fundamentals "right" prepares us for the game. I've been astounded by friends and business leaders who are working on complex scenarios involving acquisitions or international partnerships when the business in front of them was crumbling around them. The fundamentals were not taught, not practiced, and ultimately, not known by the team that was expected to win the big games in the current market. These may be simple concepts, but they take constant vigilance to maintain and propagate.

Leaders, if we do just these two things, I predict an amazing thing will happen within our organizations: VITALITY will be restored. Vital literally means "life." When they take your vital signs at the hospital, they are checking to be sure you are still alive—are there signs of life in the body? Organizations have vital signs, too, and I have not seen any truly vital organizations that lack either vision or values. Mathematically, I think it looks like this:

VISION + VALUES = VITALITY.

It takes both vision and values to achieve organizational vitality. We may have a very noble vision, but if we are willing to be dishonest, if we lack compassion, if the humans in the organization do not grow as a result of our vision, there can be no vitality. Conversely, we may have wonderful values, but if we've decided that our vision is "to enhance shareholder value" or some other statement that can be understood as substantially self-serving or downright ignoble, it will be impossible to achieve workplace vitality. (Is it possible to have a positive culture in a crack house—really?)

Back to the fundamental questions: What do I truly desire from my work life, and am I happy with the person I am becoming? As leaders, it's both a personal question AND a team question. It's part of our fundamental responsibility.

Is it worth the effort required to articulate our vision and values? It's reasonable to ask, but what's the alternative? Are there cracks in the foundation that will let the house fall? Is there deadwood in the organization? How did it get there? There is no better antidote than strong leadership to address these issues. If you're still with me, let's talk about these in more detail.

CHAPTER 8:
VISION

"Where there is no vision, the people perish."
Proverbs 29:18 KJV

For many years, our local newspaper carried the above quotation in the masthead of its publication. Front and center—a biblical quotation in as politically incorrect place as you could hope to find—the Pulliam family who owned and published the paper made their paper's mission and vision fully transparent. The social conscience aspect of journalism was, and is, an important element of our free society. But more importantly, this "truth statement" from the history of the Hebrew people caught the essence, the true vision, of the Pulliam press. This was an exercise in journalism that was intended to cast a vision. This was no mere daily newspaper. This was, according to their masthead, a matter of life and death! Pretty compelling reason to go to work, don't you agree?

A good friend of mine owns several limestone quarries. Mining huge blocks of monument-quality Indiana limestone from Mother Earth—who is always stubborn to give it up—is an incredible operation. The process begins with careful mapping of the geology, which requires hundreds of core samples to be taken from across hundreds of acres. Excavation, blasting, more excavation, diamond-studded saws that are fifteen feet long cutting long ribbons into the earth, driving wedges into the earth at just the right depths to cause the rock to break loose along natural stress lines, and then the real work of harvesting begins! The stone is manually split again with wedges to workable dimensions, and then huge loaders grab the raw limestone to hoist it onto material handling trucks where each stone is carefully measured, marked, and stored for future use. Finally, when a new job calls for specific cuts of stone, the craftsmen choose from their limestone orchard the right pieces of stone for each job. Carefully, painstakingly, the raw stones are turned into machined and milled finished stone for some of the world's most spectacular buildings, including the Pentagon of the United States government, the Empire State Building, and the National Cathedral in Washington, D.C.

What impressed me more than the raw logistics of mining the stone was the energy with which the crews literally danced across the quarry. With some manufacturing background in my bones, I was amazed at the manufacturing process. But with my interest in organizational development, I couldn't help but comment to my friend about this incredibly positive work ethic among people who were doing difficult, dangerous, and dirty work. His response, which was fully evident throughout their offices where pictures of their signature works were proudly displayed on every wall, was, "We're not mining limestone, Wil. We're building monuments!"

How is a quarrying operation like a software company (our company), and like your company? It's not *what* we're doing that gives energy and drive to an organization. It's *why* we're doing it! Vision captures the "why" of every organization. Appropriately cast, every person in the organization can link their jobs directly to it, and in so doing, their work, indeed their lives, derive purpose and nobility. Those are lofty claims, and I masked a difficult task with the simple words, "appropriately cast," but I believe those claims are true, and I believe it is the first responsibility of leadership.

As we mentioned in Part I, in the '80s, strategic planning with its incumbent attention on mission statements and goals swept the business community. This was, in fairness, a transformational event for many organizations as it brought focus and clarity to businesses that had substantially evolved rather than growing toward an intentional identity. Unfortunately, it seemed that many businesses began to do more than run their operations according to the plan. For many, these carefully constructed blueprints became public relations pieces, with the primary audience being the stockholders or Wall Street. Regardless of the reason, many companies allowed their foundational statement of mission, their *raison d'etre,* to become as simple, and as uninspiring, as "enhance shareholder value." Try to imagine how motivating that is for any of the other stakeholders who are not shareholders. From that perspective, what we have just adopted as the reason for living (at least at work) is to make more money for people who are undoubtedly perceived as already having more money than God! Doesn't that just fire up your engines in the morning!

There is no shortcut for developing a great mission statement. I've given examples of two in the introduction to this chapter. At Ontario Systems, I mentioned earlier that our mission statement used to be a combination of mission and philosophy. We have separated those now, and we use our vision and value statements to express our corporate philosophy. So, how does it look in that structure?

Mission: Our mission is to be the Receivables Management Information System provider of choice worldwide.

Vision: Our vision is to change the world of Receivables Management.

Values: See the Statement of Corporate Philosophy discussed in Part I.

For us, this is just the latest evolution of these various understandings. We like what they do for us, but I am sharing them only as examples, and make no particular claim as to how good they are or how well you might be able to model your particular statements following ours.

The virtue of our current mission statement is that it:

1) Focuses on a market (Receivables Management, worldwide, first-party and third-party entities);

2) Describes a quality component (provider of choice—excellence!);

3) Gives direction for future decisions (say "no" to non-RMIS work, say "yes" to international).

That tells us what the business does. We have additional strategy statements that undergird this mission statement with operational directives, but everything ties back to this organizational imperative.

The virtue of our current vision statement is that:

1) We can help every person in our organization understand how they play a role in this transformational work;

2) "Changing the world" for the better in a very tough industry calls us to serve every component of our markets in meaningful ways. From the telephone agent to the owner, from the credit grantor to the end customer, we can help people restore integrity to the credit process in a very efficient and effective way. Because we empathize with the challenge of the work our customers do, we have a sense of urgency about getting it done sooner rather than later. Our vision for them is tantamount to leadership—helping

them to see their potential in our "new world" so clearly that they are inspired to achieve it.

Each organization will need to derive its own, inspirational (breathing life into) vision statement. Once defined, it takes even more effort to evangelize the vision to every person. But once evangelized, if you marry the vision to appropriate values, you will almost certainly see the vital signs of your organization begin to pulsate with energy and enthusiasm. In my experience, people want to believe what they are doing is important. We need to help them see that it truly is!

CHAPTER 9:
VALUES

"Values are the gutter guards down the bowling lane of life."
                                              Wil Davis

In Part I of this book, we discussed values that work, a set of values that have been engaged in a real-world setting for over twenty years. Although we agreed that these are not necessarily the only values, we offered them by way of example so that you might be encouraged to articulate your own set of values and to begin setting the course for creating an intentional corporate culture.

We named each of the paragraphs of our Statement of Corporate Philosophy with a one-word mnemonic that encapsulated the foundational value being extolled in each paragraph. The five values were: Stewardship, Integrity, Service, Tolerance (or Respect for the Individual), and Professionalism. In this section, I want to revisit those values and discuss what they mean from a leadership perspective. Remember, as leaders, we will be held to higher standards, so there are some unique perspectives that I think are helpful as we strive to become more effective leaders for our teams.

Stewardship

The first value was stewardship. From a leadership or managerial perspective, I believe stewardship is all about dealing with people. As we discussed in the introduction to the term stewardship, some people seem to think that stewardship applies primarily to money or material resources. Perhaps this is where the helpful distinction can be made that we manage things, and we provide leadership to people. Money, capital budgets, and physical resources are, by economic theory, all relatively scarce resources that we must manage in order to maximize their effective use. People, on the other hand, are not a fixed entity. You don't find people in nice, neat piles of denominations like you do money. People grow, change, react, and interact. Being a good steward of our leadership responsibilities means helping the people on our teams grow, change, react, and interact in increasingly healthy and productive ways.

Some may get only this far before wanting to raise their hands and object. "Hey, I'm not the babysitter. We're tasked to get a job done. I don't want to work on all this soft, fuzzy stuff." And to those who might tend in that direction, let me share this observation. I believe that:

**Substantive and sustainable corporate growth
is predicated on
substantive and sustainable personal growth.**

I have observed short-term growth produced by mergers or acquisitions, but if the cultures of the two companies are not assimilated well, the merger can disintegrate into a disaster. If we are primarily interested in creating long-term, sustainable organizations, there is simply no substitute for building into the lives of our people—building capacity, competency, and even character whenever possible. Overall, good stewardship of the organization is absolutely equivalent to good stewardship of the people in the organization. That's what this section, directed to leadership responsibilities in the area of stewardship, is focused on encouraging.

One of the keys to being an effective leader is to ask ourselves the right questions in the various circumstances we face. When thinking about being a steward of our people resources, I think the key question is this: "What is the best, 'next thing' for this person to experience?" Graphically, I see this as a continuous circle of experience, where we think about:

1) Opportunity—What's the next experience in which we can engage the whole person so that he or she can continue to grow?

2) Responsibility—What can I do to help her or him fully "own" responsibility for this opportunity?

3) Authority—Have I fully empowered the associate with appropriate authority so that she or he can complete this assignment well?

4) Accountability—Have we agreed upon metrics of timing and deliverables that will help us both measure the progress?

This becomes a repeating cycle of opportunities and experiences where our associate has the opportunity to become everything he or she was created to be. Our task as leaders is to provide these opportunities.

Frankly, I find it relatively easy to do steps 1, 2, and 3 of this cycle. I genuinely enjoy observing growth in my friends and colleagues. It's exciting for both of us to share the confidence and positive expectations that each new project implies, and it's always great when the projects are completed on time and under budget! However, in the real world, step 4 is incredibly important precisely because projects tend to be late and over budget! We're going to devote an entire section of the book to the general topic of accountability, but I can confess even before we get there that if there is an area in which it is very easy to fail as a leader, it is in this area of accountability.

By the way, in order to be a good steward of your own gifts, talents, and abilities, I would encourage you to develop an opportunity list for yourself. Where do you need to develop? What kinds of opportunities would be helpful to that development? Where will you find mentors? Have you identified someone to whom you will submit for both personal and professional accountability? There is simply no substitute for personal growth. My suspicion is that the ultimate purpose for each of us to be born was to grow to become something more than who we currently are. With a little thought and intention, we can help to move ourselves along in the process!

Integrity

The second value was integrity, and from a leadership perspective, I believe this value is most effectively modeled by personal example. Again, just because we are in leadership positions, we will be scrutinized more closely by others. Two questions that help leaders think about this important responsibility might be:

1) What will people perceive from my example?

2) Is this truly fair for all parties?

At one time or another, we all experience the frustrating results of the difference between real integrity and perceived integrity. As leaders, we absolutely must maintain our real integrity, and we must become very sensitive to the way perceived integrity can undermine our leadership.

Several years ago, one of our senior sales guys came back from a road trip and submitted his expense report. Stapled to the expense report was an empty bag of peanuts and a $4 "cheap seat" ticket to a Cincinnati Reds baseball game. Clearly marked under "dinner" on the expense report was the $4 ticket plus the $1.75 bag of peanuts for $5.75. I was amused at my friend's creativity, and I was more than pleased to sign off on the expense report because I was sure that this would have been the least expensive meal this guy would ever buy! I had signed it and was just about to send it to the accounting department when I stopped and realized that his perceived integrity was at risk. Why would I think so?

In spite of the fact that he had been very direct and honest about his expenditure, this expense report was moving from the hands of a person who travels between eighty and a hundred nights per year on behalf of the company, across my desk to someone who has never traveled even one time on company business. How might this good-natured "meal" expense be perceived under those circumstances?

"Hey, look at this! I have to work for a living, but the company pays for him to fly all over the country and now he's even getting us to pay for his baseball games and refreshments. Where do I get a job like that?!"

Perhaps that's an exaggeration, but at least I recognized that the stage was set for a misunderstanding. So, I attached an explanatory note to the report, acknowledging why I believed it was both honest and good stewardship to allow this particular expense, and it was a true non-event.

Importantly, did my friend have a problem with integrity? Absolutely not. Might he have had a problem with perceived integrity? Absolutely. The best antidote for this problem is to simply stop and ask, "What will others perceive from my example?"

The other question is really helpful when leaders are making decisions on behalf of the team. "Is this truly fair for all parties?" will steer us away from giving ourselves or a subset of the organization what may be perceived as a self-serving privilege. Frankly, company award programs are very susceptible to being perceived as "unfair," especially if only a select few have the opportunity to be recognized. It is still an interesting phenomenon to me that so many companies have separate Sales Award Trips to exotic locations, when no other department in the company even has an annual awards dinner. In every circumstance where I have personally known the company with such a policy, it has undermined teamwork both within the department and across the company. It's fun for a few, it's easy to include ourselves as leaders, and it builds walls that are both thick and tall. Is it truly fair for all parties? One measure is simply, can all parties participate? While many people will find this standard difficult enough that they will not want to give up their parking spot by the door, separate restroom facilities, etc., if we want to be effective leaders, we will derive most of our influence from personal character rather than a position on an organization chart. Leading by personal example is a prerequisite to personal authority, and that's the real key to effective leadership.

Service

As a leader in a culture that celebrates the key value of service, our perspective is one of servant leadership. You recall that this keyword was derived from studying the leadership style of Jesus, someone who exemplified good stewardship and integrity while building a spectacular organization. His simple formula: to be the greatest of all, you must become a servant to all. From our position as leaders, how can we best serve the needs of those we supervise? We must constantly be asking ourselves the question, "What is in our associates' best, long-term interests?" I think the greatest temptation that we will need to overcome is to substitute their short-term best interests for their long-term. It takes a fair amount of discipline, and a healthy interpersonal relationship, to provide appropriate coaching for the long-term. Frankly, it may be our short-term best interests that get sacrificed in order to allow a key team member to transfer into another department or job within the company, but if we are truly serving their best interests, we will be both encouraging and supportive of that milestone of personal growth.

I have come to believe that the reason servant leadership is so powerful is that serving others is, in effect, breathing into the lives (inspiring them) of those we serve with such positive expectations of their full potential that they become very eager to follow our suggestions for their life and career. The old saying is that "People don't care how much you know until they know how much you care." Building into the relationship allows us to influence them in both good times and difficult. When someone truly believes we have their best interests at heart, they allow themselves to be susceptible to our coaching. It just works!

What about those times when the opportunity cycle ends in obvious failure? What about the times when we've really tried to help someone achieve their potential, but for whatever reason, there is no real progress? How do we serve the other person's best interests when we feel like the work relationship is not going to work?

These are fair questions, and if our model doesn't provide solutions to the tough circumstances, it is mere platitude and Pollyannaism. What do we do in these tough circumstances?

Grounded firmly in integrity, I think we need to assess whether or not our organization with its associated opportunities is really the best "next thing" for this person to experience. Sometimes, we have collectively made an error in selection, and what we once believed was a great fit turns out to be a really poor fit for reasons beyond our original discernment. In my opinion, to stay connected to a person who cannot adequately perform the job functions required by their job assignment is not good stewardship for either the company or the individual. If we determine that is the case, carefully and with infinite respect (remember the fourth key value?), we work out a plan for separation.

Several years ago we hired a salesman whom we believed had the requisite experience, skills, and desire to learn to sell our software products. After more than two years of almost constant work and frustration trying to help this person achieve his quota, we sat down to evaluate what our next steps in coaching might be for this individual. He was frustrated. It was highly visible that he was not achieving his quotas while many others on the team were. We were frustrated due to the low performance and the high levels of energy it was taking to supervise this particular person's efforts.

In our discussion, we asked ourselves what was missing—why had he previously been successful, and why was he struggling in our environment? Ultimately, we realized that his success had been due, in large part, to the very structured nature of his prior sales work, and that the inherent ambiguity and independence of our environment was more than he knew how to manage successfully. We realized (finally) that he needed to be in a place where he could learn those skills, but we also realized that we were not structured to provide that type of training and experience for him. We were realizing that the best "next thing" for him was not in our company.

We called him in, and relived our discussion with him. He agreed that our assessment was probably at the root of his problems, but he also did not have another job lined up, so he was not anxious about losing his position with us. Ultimately, we gave him no alternative but to accept our severance offer to him—one that we believed would give him ample opportunity to find another job more suited to his skills without putting his family's security at risk. We parted company with him without parting friendship. We were convinced that his long-term best interests were being served, and this was our best way to help him become everything he was created to be.

It took a few years, but when I see this person today, he almost never fails to thank me for helping him through this important life transition! Has anyone ever thanked you for firing them? If we're truly serving others' long-term best interests, it can happen. Candidly, I'm still waiting on a few more to come back and say, "Thanks!" It may never happen. But that's what makes being grounded completely in personal integrity so important. There will be occasions when that's all we have to stand on, and we need to make sure we are on a solid foundation for those times!

Tolerance (Respect for the Individual)

You may not find this concept taught in a business school, but from a leadership perspective, I have come to believe that tolerating differences among people and infinitely respecting the diversity of created lives requires an attitude of loving other people. Of course, this is a healthy kind of non-romantic love to which my mother would refer when she would say, "You don't have to like everyone you meet, but you do have to love them!" Let's face it, that is a hard standard. When I used to work in retail banking, one of the sayings that we tellers shared was, "the only people who want to work with people are the ones who don't work with people!" People can be, well, very challenging!

So, how can we do this? What is the self-talk that helps us get past some of the irascible differences that will inevitably surface when working with people? Here are some suggestions that help me.

First, begin with the attitude that people are simply the most interesting things that were ever created, and we should enjoy them! If we start with that attitude, things that were formerly annoying, frustrating, or just plain weird can now be much more healthily described as "interesting."

Beyond "interesting," it can be very helpful to remind ourselves of the blind men and the elephant story. A very helpful question is always, "I wonder what part of the elephant they have been touching?" This helps us move toward seeking to understand more than to be understood, which builds relationships vital to having the opportunity to "breathe into" another's life at important moments. It's always good to ask, "If the roles were reversed, how would I want to be treated in this circumstance?" That's just a rephrasing of the Golden Rule, but put it to the test next time you sit down with someone in the midst of a disciplinary remediation meeting, or at the extreme, at a meeting to separate employment. How would I want to be treated? What attitude would I need to perceive in order to take this constructively? The Golden Rule is a very high standard indeed if we are willing to test it in the toughest circumstances.

Professionalism

If the value of professionalism is the capstone value that describes all the others, and if it truly means that our work "speaks before us," it should come as no surprise that I would characterize our leadership perspective on this value as simply walk the talk. If we do not have the integrity to walk the talk, we will be left to lead out of positional authority, and we will have forfeited the more compelling virtue of personal authority.

Positional authority could be simply defined as the authority derived from occupying a box on an organization chart. It is sometimes referred to as "line" authority, because this type of authority derives from the lines that connect the boxes on that same organization chart. (For example, if your box is above mine on the organization chart, and my box is connected to yours by a line, you will be deemed to have authority over me.)

Personal authority, on the other hand, can be thought of as the intersection of personal character and personal competence. Regardless of the box occupied on an organization chart, people with high character and high competence will command inordinate authority by virtue of these compelling personal characteristics.

As leaders, if we find ourselves leading primarily from positional authority, the chances are pretty good that we are not particularly effective leaders. Conversely, if we primarily manage out of personal authority, we are probably very effective leaders, indeed.

It is not possible to shortcut personal authority. One needs both character and competence. Someone of very high personal character who is professionally incompetent will never be followed. We might enjoy an evening of bowling with them, but we wouldn't want to follow them in our career pursuits. Similarly, someone who is incredibly competent, but with little personal character, will not inspire enough trust to engage people as followers. We might, although often reluctantly, consult with them about a "bits and bytes" question of technology, but we will also not want to be supervised by that type of person. However, when the constellation of character and competence comes into alignment, one can be a tremendously effective leader without title or position.

Occasionally, a company will recognize that it has a very competent technician who has become somewhat of a prima donna. You know the type—convinced that he or she is, indeed, our most invaluable employee. Based on our discussion so far, what do you think I might suggest would be a really good, "next thing" for a prima donna to experience? How about the fact that our organization really can get along without them? If you have one (or more) of these types in your company, I know that right now you're weighing your short-term pain against this suggestion for their, and the company's, long-term gain, but we know that it's the right thing to do for both the individual and the company. We might be amazed and surprised at the creativity and energy we unleash in the organization when we step up to this intellectual bully on our team!

There is one more insight that I would like to share on what it means to be a professional from a leadership perspective. Let me begin by telling you a true story that I found difficult to understand until I was a junior in college.

My twin brother and I are nothing alike—fraternal twins, different interests, different personalities, etc. We are very close personally, but very different human beings, too. When we were in high school, our dad, who is a minister, accepted a call to a church in a different community, and we moved to a new school during the last two grading periods of our junior year. This was, by sheer coincidence, about the time that school elections occurred for the following year. Although we were new to the community and the school, my brother and another friend were elected president and vice president of every organization in the school—and even our youth group at church. Both of these guys are very likable, but their sheer domination of all the school leadership positions really surprised me! After all, if you were choosing study group team members with whom to work for a graded project, without a doubt, you would have wanted me in your group. I would get my work done, on time, and we would get an A. My brother would get most of it done before the day it was due, and the group could probably still save a B. I love my brother, but we had different work styles and priorities when it came to grades!

Sitting in a sociology class during my junior year of college, we came across a chapter on leadership styles. There was the mystery unmasked in black and white. The sociologists refer to two kinds of leadership styles: task and social. A task-oriented leader tends to get things accomplished by increasing the stress, turning up the temperature so to speak, until they get the project boiling quickly and accomplish the task. Getting something accomplished is their primary value, and the primary way in which they feel good about themselves. A socially oriented leader gets things accomplished relationally. When the stress is building, a social leader tells a joke! When the study group is working late at night against an 8 A.M. deadline, the social leader will suggest going to get a pizza! Clearly, I am a recovering task-oriented leader! My brother is the consummate socially oriented leader. When I realized what was going on, and how effective each leadership style was for different circumstances, I began to see how incredibly powerful it would be if those of us who suffer with being task oriented could adopt the style of socially oriented leaders. Conversely, for those who are burdened with being a socially oriented leader, it would be powerfully synergistic for them to adopt some of the virtues of getting a task done like task-oriented leaders do so naturally. Both styles bring a gift to an organization—

task leaders get things done; social leaders make it fun to get things done. Putting them together will unlock tremendous potential in the organization and provide a sustainable model of leadership that others will acclaim as truly professional!

Synthesis

Leadership: How do I do it?

I agree, this is hard work! But I believe you will agree, it's definitely worth it. In the final analysis, maybe we can boil this down to three principles to guide our leadership efforts.

1) Inspire Others—Breathe into their lives the potential we see until they see it so clearly that they are inspired and determined to achieve it! This will require a personal investment of caring and nurturing, but the paradox to that process is that in caring for and nurturing others, we will be cared for and nurtured ourselves. It's a wonderfully "growthy" place to be!

2) Serve Others—Relentlessly and ruthlessly pursue serving the other person's best, long-term interests. Think about leaders who have inspired you: parents, teachers, coaches, friends. Honestly, wasn't it their incessant expectation that you could succeed that ultimately persuaded you to invest of yourself in achieving whatever that goal truly was? We must believe in other people, and serving them well is the best vote of confidence we can give.

3) Lead Others—If we will invest in other people by inspiring the very best in them, if we will serve them by helping them become fully all that they were created

to be, an amazing thing will happen. When we turn around, we'll notice that they are following us. The most important thing I will say about leadership is this: *It's the by-product, not the goal.* People who jump to the front of the line rarely make great leaders. People who are pushed to the front by the people in whom they have invested by their service are already the real leaders. It's not a matter of personal charisma. It's a matter of putting others first!

Can we do this? If we could, would it make a real difference? My answer to those questions is an emphatic YES! I love the quote from Margaret Mead, the world-famous anthropologist who spent her entire career—her calling—studying the peoples and people groups of the world. Her conclusion is worth remembering:

"Never doubt that a small group of thoughtful, committed citizens can change the world. It is, indeed, the only way it has ever been done!"

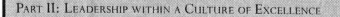

Discussion and Reflection Questions

1) Tell about someone whom you have admired as a great leader. Why did you allow them to lead you?

2) To what extent do you think leadership is an inherited trait vs. a learned trait?

3) List those whom you influence at this stage in your life. (Remember your many roles!) What one thing could you focus on to become a more effective leader?

4) Is it possible to lead those who are leading you? Explain.

PART III:

---

*Accountability—Keeping
the Integrity of the Culture*

CHAPTER 10:
ACCOUNTABILITY—KEEPING THE CULTURE

A positive and productive corporate culture may be the business equivalent to the Holy Grail. Pursuit of the elusive object has its own rewards, while achieving it and holding on to it can seem transient at best.

At this point in our discussion, we have considered the values on which a culture of excellence can be built. We have discussed the unique role of leadership in establishing and nurturing that culture. But a question remains that we should explore. How do you keep the integrity of the culture? Can we really hold onto the Holy Grail?

In my experience, a corporate culture is a relatively fragile thing. The passing of time can seem to weaken it. Inattention to small details can leave the whole culture relegated to the status of a quaint experiment that has lost its relevance. As insidious and subtle as time and inattention can be, a tidal wave force that puts pressure on the integrity of a corporate culture is simply size. The organization can fall victim to its own success! As with computer systems, in organizational systems, size will break things. Computer systems that work well with thirty users will be fatally flawed for three hundred. Human systems that work at one size will demonstrate similar fatal flaws when the size of the organization changes dramatically. While an individual's force of personality, or even that of a small group, may keep the culture together for a long time, in my experience, somewhere past three hundred persons, no one person or leadership group will be able to hold it together. Why is that? All the informal systems that make possible keeping the culture up to that size will begin to fail. For example, with increased size, it is no longer possible to know everyone's name. We can no longer speak to everyone in the company every day. We may no longer be in the same physical building or town. All these barriers to communication insure that no one person or leadership group can sustain a culture, regardless of their personal abilities and charisma. What's the solution?

We have become convinced that the long-term solution is to insure that the entire workforce is empowered to exercise mutual accountability with each other. If we're going to open that door, we will need to be explicit about the things to which we will be held accountable. Here's a list that I think makes sense.

- **Job**—Whatever the work elements are for a position, we should all agree that we are accountable to each other for the professional execution of those responsibilities.

- **Relationships**—It's not often written into a job description, but one unarticulated expectation that most employers have for their teams is that they play nicely together in the sandbox. There is no reason to let resentments fester. We need to hold each other accountable to always be working toward resolving relational issues.

- **Attitudes**—People who have chronically bad attitudes need our help and encouragement. As miserable as it makes us to be around them, imagine how much more miserable they are living with themselves! We owe each other positive attitudes!

- <u>Self</u>—In short, we are accountable for our very selves! While we may not have a direct accountability responsibility for our teammates when they leave work, there is no doubt that what we do in other hours of our lives can impact our working hours. When we say we will hold each other accountable, and this is extremely important, we mean that we will hold each other accountable to that person's best understanding of what it means to be a good *steward*, with *integrity*, by being of *service*, and by *respecting other people*. Particularly in this area of accountability for self, we need to be infinitely respectful of each other, not imposing our ideas of what stewardship implies personally for any other individual. Those decisions are their responsibility! (See paragraph four of the Statement of Corporate Philosophy.)

- <u>Vision and Values</u>—In simplified form, aren't we really saying that each of us bound together in this special community we call "our work" is accountable to each other for achieving our Vision within the exercise of our Values? That's what I think it means, and being mutually accountable for that seems only fair.

In discussing this concept with many groups over the years, I have been able to generate a fairly lively discussion by postulating the following: All performance deficiencies are, ultimately, a breach of corporate values. In other words, when we find ourselves in a position of needing to provide coaching (accountability) to a fellow employee on a particular issue, at the root of the circumstance will be a breach of corporate values.

Everyone can agree about any circumstance involving willful misbehavior—obviously, that lacks integrity, is poor stewardship, and is probably providing poor service. The situations that are less obvious are the ones where a person is honestly trying to do the job, but lacks specific skills or abilities to actually perform the task. There may be an exception, but when this type of circumstance occurs, there is probably a selection error on the front end of the employment process that did not permit either the company or the candidate to realize that they lacked such a skill or ability. Is such a circumstance also a breach of corporate values? I think the argument can be made that it is. Given that the company is doing a good job of providing feedback along the way, the employee is probably well aware of the performance shortfall and is probably personally frustrated by it. This honest, well-meaning person is undoubtedly reluctant to admit that they don't have the skills or abilities to do the job, but they are in a very tough position. I would argue that it is probably not good stewardship on their part to stay involved in a position where they are unprepared to be successful. They can either find another job within the company that does not contain the job elements they are unable to perform, or they can find another position outside the company. We have had these very circumstances occur. Because we accept our responsibility for the selection error on the front end, we try to make sure there is an adequate transition "safety blanket" for the employee and his or her family in terms of compensation and benefits, and we try to help the individual get back to a personally and professionally satisfying position where he or she can be fully successful rather than trying to fit the proverbial square peg in a round hole. It's the best next thing for the individual, and therefore, for the company.

In my view, all performance coaching should have as its goal remediation, not termination. Remediation will almost always require growth, and growth in employees is absolutely key to growth in the company. Remember the truism that we noted in Chapter 9 when we discussed the value of stewardship: Substantive and sustainable corporate growth is predicated on substantive and sustainable personal growth. For most of us, that growth requires healthy accountability.

There are two specific verses of scripture that speak to this issue of accountability. (Undoubtedly there are more, but I think these two provide a nice framework for thinking about the subject with some wisdom on our side.) The first verse comes from the wisdom literature of the Old Testament, from the book of Proverbs where the author notes, "as iron sharpens iron, so one man (person) sharpens another" (Proverbs 27:17). It's one of those verses that, in all honesty, I really don't like. It makes accountability sound so brutal, conflictive, painful! The balancing verse for this one is, in my opinion, taken from the New Testament letters where the author is writing to a fledgling organization in Ephesus, and he encourages the members of that organization to "speak the truth in love" (Ephesians 4:15). That seems like a wonderfully balanced picture to me. In ancient times, iron was sharpened by hammering it with other pieces of iron. We get better when we allow others to sharpen us. But if words are our hammers, how should they be spoken? According to the writer of Ephesians, they should always be spoken "in love." I know that many of us are committed to "speaking the truth," so that part is not really the hardest part. However, speaking the truth and having it received "in love" is a much more difficult proposition. We can adopt the goal in a moment, but it will take a lifetime to master the craft!

What are the risks of having poor accountability systems in an organization? You can probably add to my list, but here are things I've observed:

1) Without accountability, humans can tend toward slothfulness. Slothfulness is another word for laziness. If we are honest with ourselves, sometimes we might stop short of excellence if mediocre seems OK. Achieving our best often requires a healthy tension that accountability can provide.

2) Without accountability, misperceptions will persist that will ultimately lead to resentment. In your own experience, in the absence of communication to the contrary, does it seem to you that human nature always assumes the best about situations? My experience is that humans seem to assume the worst more often than not. It's not fair, and it's not right, but it is reality. Without accountability, we lack the awareness to correct the misperceptions. This can be one of the real gifts of accountability to any organization.

3) Without accountability, persons may remain in the state of "unconscious incompetence." You may be familiar with the four stages of acquiring any skill. We begin as "unconscious incompetents"—we simply don't know what we don't know. When someone tells us about our unconscious incompetence, we move to the level of "conscious incompetent"—at least we now know what we didn't know! Deciding to acquire the skill, we determine to work at accomplishing the task, and with a great deal of effort, we learn we can do it! At this stage, we are "consciously competent"—if we think about it, we can do it. With a little practice, we can get to the place where we are "unconsciously competent." We do it without thinking about it. It has become very natural and easy—it would feel awkward to do otherwise. How I wish my golf game could get to the fourth stage!

Let me share with you a relatively trivial example from a real-world experience. I work with all kinds of personalities. Some are stereotypical, so without offending any of you who are in this category but don't fit the stereotype, let me just say that, in my experience, accountants, programmers, and engineers are quite often of a low social vector personality. They don't need lots of social affirmation, and consequently, they don't give much. When these people matriculate into positional leadership responsibilities and begin to supervise other people, invariably they will have some folks who work with them who have higher social needs. I have literally found it necessary to encourage these personality types to simply "smile more." When the idea is first mentioned, you can tell that they are unconscious incompetents. That is one idea that has never occurred to them! Why would I just smile more? (And they always think this thought with a very serious look on their face!) Of course, the reason is that the people with whom they work are watching, looking for clues about how "the boss" is doing (remember, you will be held to a higher standard just because you are a "boss") and "connecting the dots" between what they see and what they have experienced before, most likely in other places of employment. When the "boss" smiles, everyone relaxes a little and can enjoy a more productive day. As my accounting, programming, or engineering friends work at it, they can become consciously competent very quickly. Although it may take a long time to smile spontaneously, it is amazing what this one little "tip" can do for morale across a department or organization. But, until someone informs us that it would be helpful to do, we are likely to remain unconscious incompetents and spread an unintentional negative perception throughout the company.

With such important negative consequences caused by lack of accountability, why doesn't everyone seek it out? I think there are some deeply imbedded concerns that people have regarding accountability. Whether we learned them in our family of origin, at school, or in other places of work, here are some of the common reasons that people resist accountability:

1) Somebody will be mad—We believe that if we hold people accountable, they will likely respond to us out of embarrassment, disappointment, or anger. Their frustration will cause them to behave as though they are mad at us, and that is a risk we just don't want to take.

2) Risk of open conflict or alienation—If someone is mad, then there is a risk that we will become involved in either an argument (the fight response) or alienation (the flight response). At the very least, the conflict speaks of a deeper level of frustration, and we worry that we will be more likely to have a conflict in the future if we risk one now.

3) All conflict is bad—This is a myth, but it is a pervasive one. The opposite is true: Well-managed conflict is healthy. We grow from it, we get better because of it, and we mature as humans from multiple cycles of the process.

Although each of these concerns may have different root causes or varying degrees of validity, all are really excuses that prevent us from growing as individuals, and therefore, from growing as an organization. Remember, without accountability, there are real problems. The downward spiral of unresolved conflict, which leads to resentment or bitterness, and ultimately results in broken relationships, has no end without the skills of accountability, which can both stop the spiral and heal the conflict.

At the end of this section, I will ask everyone to make a personal commitment to accountability. Right now, this may seem like too much to ask, but after we discuss both the attitudes and skills associated with healthy accountability, I have confidence you will be able to make this commitment. For now, all I want to do is to set out the commitment and allow you to consider it as we discuss the tools we need to do this well. The commitment I will ask for is this:

Beginning today, we will care enough about each other to hold each other accountable!

Ultimately, I don't think we can claim to genuinely care about each other, maybe even ourselves, if we don't seek healthy accountability in our lives. We can't say we care about someone and then allow them to continue in self-defeating, self-sabotaging, or self-limiting behaviors. We can't say we care about the organization and then insulate ourselves from doing anything but our best work. As part of any community, this may be the fundamental commitment. Unfortunately, in many businesses, it has become the last commitment that is traditionally made!

CHAPTER 11:
RECEIVING ACCOUNTABILITY

To the extent that most of us agree that accountability is important, when we begin to think about including it in our corporate cultures, I think we generally begin by thinking about holding someone else accountable. For purposes of our discussion, I want to begin by talking about the times when someone holds us accountable. The important questions that will help guide our thinking are: What should my attitude be when someone holds me accountable, and what should I say and/or do?

Of course, at this point, there is some leader who is thinking of skipping ahead to the next chapter on giving accountability. In their minds, the idea of receiving accountability may be a quaint idea, but it is irrelevant to them—they're the boss!

To those contemplating that move, please don't! In order for us to maintain the integrity of our culture, it is important to lead by example, to create systems that are truly fair for all parties, and that will be perceived as having the whole team's best interests at heart. For accountability to accomplish its work, it must be a fully mutual responsibility shared by every member of the staff. It's not a privilege for the staff, it's a responsibility. We owe it to each other—we care enough about each other—to truly help each other by holding ourselves accountable. So, to the positional leaders reading at this point, I'm asking you to hang in there. It will be worth it!

It's not enough to simply say, "Yes, we encourage mutual accountability. If someone has a problem, they can talk to me about it." In my view, the minimum ante to be able to say you are really in the game of mutual accountability is a 360-degree appraisal process. That means that every year, every person who is in a supervisory role receives a performance appraisal from not only their direct supervisor, but from everyone they supervise, and even selected peers in the organization. Every supervisory person in our company receives this feedback every year, and it's an incredibly healthy process.

By way of encouraging you to implement this in your organization, let me share a very personal, quite painful, and somewhat embarrassing experience from my own life. In my first career job at the bank, I was hired to supervise the accounting department, which was comprised of people with seniority ranging from seven years to thirty-plus years. I was twenty-one years old, a new college graduate, and I had no clue what an unconscious incompetent I was! The training program consisted of allowing each of the accounting staff to teach me their particular jobs so that I would be able to backfill for them when they went on vacation or needed to be off work. Predictably, at least one person in the group thought they should have been selected for my position, and all the others generally agreed. How many of you know from this brief description that this was going to be a tough assignment?!

After a few months of working together, it seemed to me that I was learning most of the job elements, but it was very clear that we were anything but a team. I had very limited success engaging any of my teammates in substantive conversation (eyes rolled, sarcasm abounded, etc.), so I hit upon the idea of allowing them to provide me an anonymous evaluation. I wrote four broad questions addressing their perceptions of strengths, weaknesses, areas to work on, etc., and I shared the idea with my supervisor, who was an officer of the bank. His advice was simple: "I wouldn't do that. You will probably not like what you read, and then you'll have to figure out what to do about it. I wouldn't do that."

Well, he didn't say not to do it, so I did it anyway. (That's the great part about being twenty-one—sometimes you just don't know what good advice really is!)

I called a meeting, explained that I wanted to know how I was doing from their point of view, gave them a week to complete the documents, and explained how they could get them to me anonymously by using an envelope on the departmental secretary's desk. No one turned their work in early, but as they left for the weekend on Friday night, all of them managed to sneak their work into the envelope.

I was very anxious to read what they said. It just couldn't be as bad as I thought it was, could it? Actually, it was worse. I had invited their best shots, and they had taken them. There was very little feedback on job elements, and there was an encyclopedic listing of personal stuff. For example, there was a dress code at the bank that included a line stating that "foundation garments shall not be visible." As a new college graduate, I was actually a fairly stylish dresser, and I had a pair of bright yellow bell-bottom pants (I see you turning green with envy already!) that were both expensive and stylish. It never occurred to me that it was possible to discern a "foundation garment" line through those pants—what are you lookin' at, anyway—but to my associates, each time I wore those pants I was flaunting the dress code policy, my position as a supervisor, God, motherhood, and apple pie!

I spent the entire weekend thinking—hurting, aching, feeling sorry for myself—about those assessments. I did not have another job lined up, or I think I would have quit before Monday morning. I'm pretty sure that they were hoping that might happen! But Monday morning, I showed up at the regular time, and so did they.

So, I called a quick departmental meeting. I thanked them for taking time to document their thoughts, and more importantly, their feelings. I pledged to work on the things I could—I promised never to wear the yellow pants again—and I told them that since this evaluation was so revealing and I had so much work to do, that we would be doing it again in six months. I pointed out to them that I had not hired myself, and I understood that they did not hire me, either. However, I was committed to doing the best job I could, and their feedback was going to help me get better, so I was, again, thankful.

We ended the meeting within five minutes of its start.

It didn't happen immediately, but little by little, over a six-month period, something miraculous happened. The boil that had been lanced healed. It healed so completely that when I left the bank about a year later, you would have thought they were losing a brother. Ironically, I have the privilege of serving as the chairman of that bank today, and it is still amazing to me that some of my best friends at the bank are those with whom I worked in the accounting department when I first started work.

Using a 360-degree tool well is important. I liken it to customer relations. The customer is not always right, but the customer is always the customer. The feedback may not always be right, but it is the best representation you can get of the feelings and perceptions that are driving your team. We went from fragmented to cohesive—from barely functioning to tackling huge conversions and backlogs as a team with incredible effectiveness. Although I was fortunate to have apparently chosen a good strategy relating to the information I collected, today I would counsel folks that it's important to get some help discerning how best to utilize the information. It can be a true gold mine, full of nuggets that you will not be able to mine any other way.

From this story, perhaps you have already discerned what I believe our attitudes should be regarding receiving accountability feedback. I believe our highest response should be based on gratitude. What would our normal tendencies be? When I received such caustic feedback, I think it took me the entire weekend of personal reflection, even prayer, to sort out my anger, defensiveness, denial, and a whole host of unhealthy responses. In the end, I came to believe that gratitude was the only reasonable response. I had asked for it, they had delivered.

Gratitude makes sense for other reasons, too. Receiving feedback means somebody cares enough about me to give it. The accounting staff could have answered with one-word answers or single sentences. Each one wrote a book! Down deep, they must have wanted it to work to make such an investment. Gratitude makes sense because it is clear that someone believes in us. Taking the time to give us candid feedback is one way of saying, "I believe you can do better, and I believe you want to do better." What a wonderful gift!

Perhaps from my story you also discerned a pattern that will help to answer the question, "What do I do?" Each time we receive feedback from our performance, positive or negative, we can exercise what John Miller calls a QBQ Moment. From his book, *The Question Behind the Question*, Miller proposes constructing a simple sentence with three parts:

1) All QBQ's begin with "What" or "How"

2) All QBQ's contain an "I"

3) All QBQ's focus on action

Putting these elements together into a helpful phrase might sound like this: "What or how can I help, serve, build, improve, achieve, etc.?" The focus is always on us and our response. Questions that begin with "Why" or "When" or most other words will ultimately seem to be shifting the blame to other persons. Staying with "What" or "How" linked with "I" allows us to work on our part in any dilemma. In Miller's book, he reminds us of the familiar Serenity Prayer, which says, "God, grant me the serenity to accept the things I cannot change, the courage to change the things I can, and the wisdom to know the difference." When using QBQ's, Miller suggests a new version of the prayer which I think is perfect for receiving accountability in a healthy way: "God grant me the serenity to accept the *people* I cannot change, the courage to change the *one* I can, and the wisdom to know. . . it is *me!*"

On a personal note, I think it important to recognize the broader application of this principle. There are many people who would like to "breathe into" our lives, give us feedback that would help us, and encourage us along the journey. Many of them are within your family setting—parents, siblings, spouse, and even your children. For most of us, all it might require to astound and amaze these dear ones in our lives would be for us to adopt an attitude of gratitude when they give us feedback that we might not like to hear. Watch the genuine surprise splash across their faces when you simply say, "Thanks, I want to do that better, too. I appreciate your willingness to help me in this area." Are we willing to allow our spouses and children to shape us? Seek them out. Check out their feelings. Then exercise a QBQ moment. Not only will you be building stronger and better relationships with those you genuinely love the most, you'll be modeling a life skill that will pay them dividends for the rest of their lives. It's not natural in the workplace, and my personal experience says it's even harder at home. In other words, as important as it is to exercise these attitudes and skills at work, it's even more important at home! Good luck!

CHAPTER 12:
GIVING ACCOUNTABILITY

On the other side of the coin from receiving accountability is the monumental challenge of giving accountability. Remember, it may be iron on iron that is necessary to sharpen each other, but the mandate is also to be understood as lovingly motivated. Most of us have had experiences where our best efforts seemed to fail. So, even as we approach this whole topic, we do so with appropriate humility, recognizing that there is no foolproof way to dispatch this responsibility. However, with a little practice, a little preparation, and genuine sensitivity, I'm confident we can improve our batting averages!

The first area to prepare is our own attitudes. What is the self-talk with which we set our own expectations about accountability encounters? I think there are four specific attitudes that we can cultivate to improve our skills and gain confidence in the process.

First, enter the discussion as we enter into any relationship, with an attitude of genuine caring. This is a person, probably one we've come to know fairly well, who has exhibited a behavior that can keep them from achieving their best. Somehow, I've become aware of it, and I need to care enough to want to do something about it.

(Remember the commitment I ask us to make? Here's where it gets very practical!)

Second, expect the best! There are few things in life more powerful than expectations. People will live up to positive ones, and interestingly, they will live down to negative ones. The truth is that we in the workplace are often dealing with a "wounded child" whose parents expressed such negative expectations about them throughout their childhood that getting them to "see their potential so clearly they are inspired to achieve it" is a task that can seem impossible. The good news is that people can change! When people sense our genuine high expectations, their behavior and attitudes start to change, too.

You may all know the apocryphal story (which I believe I first heard from Dr. Ron Jenson, author of *Achieving Authentic Success*) about the young teacher who was called to begin a teaching assignment mid-year in a very difficult, inner-city school. Although she was inexperienced, this young teacher seemed to work magic in her classroom, and at the teacher recognition dinner at the end of the school year, all the other teachers voted to give this new teacher (who only taught second semester) the award as the outstanding teacher in the school. When she stood to accept the award, she very humbly thanked her fellow teachers and then said something like, "if all of you would have had the outstanding students I had, you would have done just as well." The building principal came up to her after the event and asked what she had meant by her comment, because he knew that the class she had been given was a very difficult group of underachievers. She told him, "Well, if everyone's class had IQ's as high as my class, I'm sure the other teachers would have done equally well."

Confused, the principal confessed that as far as he knew, they had never taken IQ tests in that school. The young teacher insisted, "Oh

yes, they were in the grade book you gave me when I took over."
The principal asked to see the book, and when he took it, he almost
fell over backwards.

"Those aren't their IQ's—those are their locker numbers!"

How do we see the people around us? Are they bundles of limitless
potential that we'll have to really hustle to keep up with? Or are
they limited sluggards that we'll need to prod every step of the way?
On most days in the real world, the answer lies somewhere between
the two extremes. But the point is so important that we dare not
miss it. People live up to our expectations, so especially when we
are in the process of caring about them by confronting them with
an accountability message, we should check our expectations and
make sure that they are incredibly positive.

Third, we must respect each other's journey. This goes back to the
various parts of the elephant, but it gets played out in withholding
a judgment about motivation for the perceived misbehavior until
we've done all our homework. This can save us enormous personal
embarrassment. Rarely do we really have all the facts about a
situation, but our human tendency is to simply "connect the dots" of
understanding that we have from our frame of reference. Obviously,
this leaves out the other person's frame of reference, and that's the
one that really counts! As we prepare for accountability, humility is
a great antidote to keep us from behaving disrespectfully to others.
And once again, we fully expect other people to respect our point
of view—it seems the least we can do is respect the point of view
of others!

Finally, our attitude must be centered on serving the other person's
best, long-term interests. It's really not about us! It's all about,
"how can I help my associate achieve his or her full potential?"
With our own motivations grounded in serving him or her, we

come alongside our friend to help, rather than give a head-butting confrontation. Again, isn't that the attitude we would appreciate others having toward us?

Ultimately, preparing to hold another person accountable in a healthy, constructive way begins with the thought: If this person knew how their behavior affected someone else, they would want to change. Whether it's a misperception or an outright unacceptable behavior, our job is to find a way to hold the mirror appropriately, and help them look into it.

If we do this well, we invite people to receive our accountability feedback in a healthy way. They will realize, as we discussed in the last chapter, that we care for them, believe in them, and want the best for them. That is the very definition of encouragement! So, the next time we are feeling angst over a feedback session we need to have, remember, our ultimate goal is to encourage them by helping them improve their own probability of success.

Now that our attitudes are centered on the correct things, what are the mechanical skills that can help us achieve success? All of the mechanics are, at a high level, communication skills. This discussion will not be an exhaustive treatise on the many nuances of interpersonal communication. (There are many such helpful tomes in print, with my current favorite being *Crucial Conversations* by Patterson, Grenny, McMillan, and Switzler.) Like the distillation of leadership responsibilities into two primary activities, my contribution to the overall discussion on communication will be to cover the basics that will lead to success in delivering iron-sharpening messages in love.

Let me remind us all that non-verbal communication is a large and important part of the communication cycle, and the more sensitive the message to be communicated, the more important the entire environment surrounding the message. Particularly for feedback that may be in any way sensitive, selecting a neutral location that is quiet and unlikely to allow distractions is clearly optimal. Almost always, the feedback should be delivered privately, and one-on-one is often perceived as the most respectful and "friendly" way to deliver the message. Sometimes, the feedback is so sensitive, and we are insecure enough in our own skills, that we can benefit from a third-party facilitator. In those circumstances, it is typical to engage a human resource specialist in your company or one of the senior managers to be of help. I have been involved in several such circumstances over the years, and it has proven to be a "coachable" opportunity for both the giver and receiver of the accountability feedback.

Regardless of how the session is initiated, two other factors are even more important than the environment of the conversation. The first factor is timing. For all the previously discussed reasons that people are reluctant to provide accountability feedback, there seems to be a strong tendency in many persons to allow lots of time to pass between the observed event and the feedback session. Feedback doesn't necessarily need to be instantaneous—after all, we may want or need to do some serious preparation! However, in one real-life case in which I became involved, someone had been offended by someone else within weeks of being hired, and waited over fourteen years to begin the accountability process! Needless to say, after fourteen years, that issue had grown all kinds of hair, and I can tell you it never took a bath either, so it was really, really stinky! The closer to "real time" we can deal with issues, the better the memory, the less time for misperceptions to breed into resentment, and the more likely we are to "correct" a problem before it becomes persistent, larger, or accepted. Timing is very important!

The second additional factor is the most important of all. This factor consists of the actual communication skills required to have the conversation. Even after fourteen years, as mentioned in the previous example, it ultimately required communication skills to begin the process.

A very simple but incredibly flexible set of skills that I have found to be useful in many settings is taught by American Guidance Systems in their parenting curriculum called "Systematic Training for Effective Parenting" written by Don Dinkmeyer, Sr., Gary McKay, and Don Dinkemeyer, Jr. My wife and I benefited from this curriculum tremendously (both with our children and with each other!) while our children were still quite young, and the communication skills that are taught within the context of mutually respectful relationships have proven helpful in every walk of life. Let me quickly outline a few of the key skills. Once we get the basic idea for each skill, we can easily begin to imagine how they might link together and provide real, and healthy, dialogue.

I-Messages—As contrasted with "you-messages," which are inherently accusatory, blaming, and inviting of defensiveness, an "I-message" is a statement that generally begins with an I, followed by a statement about how the speaker is feeling, followed by the observation that causes the feelings. In parent-speak, "I feel discouraged when I see that your room is a mess again." In spouse-speak, "I feel frustrated and unimportant when you choose to watch *Monday Night Football* on my only night home this week." In work-speak, "I'm concerned that we won't achieve our results this quarter when our sales team is all on vacation this month." Each statement is carefully formed to accurately describe how we are feeling about a particular circumstance we are observing. I-messages are great for getting conversations started—especially the really hard ones.

<u>Reflective Listening</u>—This skill invites another person to open up to us by simply reflecting back to the person what we are observing. It is not "parroting" back to them what they have just said. [Example of parroting: Person 1 says, "It's black." Person 2 says, "What I'm hearing you say is that it's black." This trite repetition is offensive and redundant. It will finish a conversation rather than encourage one!] For example, someone slams their books on their desk rather than setting them down normally. An appropriate reflection might be, "Sounds like something has upset you?" We are letting the other person know that we have observed that something is not normal, and invited them to share more if they would like to by simply acknowledging their behavior. We don't want our reflecting to be construed as either labeling or leading—both make assumptions about the other person's character that are not ours to make! Reflective listening is also good for giving us some emotional distance in the midst of a potentially conflictive situation. For example, when someone who hasn't read this book (or any other on good communication) begins a conversation with a you-statement accusing you of something, we can sometimes disarm the person by simply reflecting back what we are hearing. For example: Unskilled person: "You always fill out these forms wrong and I have to fix them. When are you going to get it right!" Skilled person's response: "Sounds like you're pretty upset. Would you like to talk about it?" When conversations get off on the wrong foot, we can find that we need to use reflective listening repetitively, along with some interspersed I-messages, in order to salvage a constructive conversation from a potentially devastating one!

<u>Exploring Alternatives</u>—Using I-messages and reflective listening to get the issues defined and "on the table," we are now ready to begin using the skill of exploring alternatives. Exploring alternatives is simply collaborative brainstorming. It is a phase of dialogue catalyzed by open-ended questions ("What kind of things

do you think would work?" or "How do you suggest we work on this?") and mutually respectful creativity. As we exhaust our ideas for solutions, we may agree to move to the next phase of the exploration process, which is selecting a solution. It is important when selecting solutions that we pay particular attention to using other people's ideas as much as possible. The integrity of the process depends on collaboration and compromise. Thus, if we find that we are consistently using only our suggested ideas, chances are we are not truly collaborating or compromising! The last step in exploring alternatives is to summarize the agreement that we have made on our selected solution. As with the opportunity cycle discussed in Chapter 9, there seems to be a fairly normal tendency to skip this last step. It should be the safest part of the conversation— we've just brainstormed the entire range of options and agreed on a solution between ourselves. Why should this be hard? Why should it be necessary? I'm not really sure that it should be either hard or necessary, but what I do know is that unless we actually articulate the final understanding, it will amaze and confound us how many times we have understood the solution and its incumbent responsibilities differently from the person with whom we believe we have agreement. When that happens, we are setting ourselves up for another accountability session! Good communication has sometimes been summarized as a three-step process:

- Tell 'em what you're gonna tell 'em.

- Tell 'em.

- Tell 'em what you told 'em.

That may be just a bit of an overstatement, but summarizing an understanding at the end of any conversation is the only way to be sure you have an understanding at all!

<u>Looping</u>—This is not a separate skill; rather, it is an acknowledgement that in real conversations, you may loop through the skills more than once. You may have gotten to exploring alternatives, when a particular suggestion seems to ambush the conversation. To express our feelings at that point, an I-message may be helpful ("I'm anxious about the direction of this conversation."); that may need to be followed by a reflective listening statement ("It sounds as though you're really worried about this situation."); and then bringing it back to the exploring alternatives with a closed-end question ("Would you like to finish our brainstorming, or do we need to stop and talk about this issue?") Our skills can help us express ourselves in non-threatening ways, work with volatile circumstances without adding fuel to the fire, and restore dignity and respect to our relationships. Without great skills, we will simply be iron on iron—no chance to be perceived in love!

<u>Final Commitment</u>: We've discussed the attitudes, we've polished the mechanics, and now I'm ready to ask again. Will you make this commitment to mutual accountability? I know of no substitute for the personal growth that it promotes, both within us, and within those with whom we work daily.

**Beginning today, we will care enough about
each other to hold each other accountable!**

Take it to work. Share it with your team. Sign it, date it, live it. Seize the day!

Discussion and Reflection Questions

1) Tell about a time when you experienced accountability. Was it positively or negatively communicated?

2) Which part of holding others accountable do you find most difficult to imagine doing? Which part is easiest?

3) What can I do in order to become better at receiving accountability?

4) What can I do in order to become better at giving accountability?

PART IV:

Practices of the Culture

CHAPTER 13:
THE DIFFERENCE IT MAKES

From the seemingly mundane activities of recruiting new employees and compensation management systems to the exciting and unusual like a Heritage Wall and equity appreciation bonuses, a commitment to this kind of a corporate culture plays itself out in every activity, not just some, of the company's life. Once again, Ontario Systems makes no claim to have a corner on the market of good ideas on how to make sure that the corporate culture is more than words. This chapter is dedicated to providing simple ideas about some of the things that we have found helpful—inspirational—as we have sought to live up to our ideals. Even beginning this type of discussion begs for a "best practices" chat group or some other convention whereby everyone's ideas can be shared. Let me begin the discussion by sharing some of our policies and practices.

Vocabulary—Very early in the new employee orientation process, we discuss the importance of words and how we prefer to handle some words that are problematic in the workplace. To illustrate, we discourage directly the use of the term "boss" since inside the walls of work, we are all associates or colleagues. However, in spite of the fact that job titles can invite frustrating and negative comparisons among associates, they serve a reasonable purpose for customers and others on the outside of the company. For example, people on the outside may legitimately need to know to whom they can escalate a problem, and titles should help with that. My ideal hope is still to get rid of titles, but I haven't figured out how to meet the external need they serve just yet, so we maintain them. I have the same basic issue with the implications of an organization chart. However, because with size comes a need to insert accountability into communication chains as well as to help determine easily the most appropriate place within the organization where a decision should be made, we have an organization chart. It's not a very public document, but it does exist. How does this attitude of mutual respect show up in words? A simple example might be that we are fond of saying that our associates don't work *for* me or anyone else. We tell people that "you work *for* yourselves. We work *with* each other."

Another subtlety of vocabulary would include the fact that you will not find a reference to a "promotion" anywhere in our company. The word *promotion* literally means "moving forward." I think that is a pretty optimistic assessment in many circumstances where people assume new duties. Typically, one of the reasons they have been selected for a new position is because they have proven that they are competent and capable in a former position. Particularly when one steps from a technical position into a supervisory position, the move is fraught with peril. Over and over I have seen organizations "promote" their best engineer or their best salesperson into a position where they quickly prove that they are one of the worst supervisors of other humans on the planet. Of course, this creates a real problem for the company. If we have made a big deal out of the so-called promotion, the only solution is to "demote" the person. You guessed it: The word *demotion* literally means "moving down." The only way to avoid this dilemma in a culture that celebrates promotions is to discourage people from trying new jobs. Is there an alternative? One way to work around this dilemma is to announce that a person has "changed assignments," and will now be moving from outside sales to sales supervision, or from programming to programming supervisor. If supervision proves to be a bad choice for them, they simply change assignments to a position out of supervision. If there was not a big deal made of the initial change, it helps make the second change a non-event, too. There may be other solutions, but this one has worked extraordinarily well for us.

Vocabulary is incredibly important. It will belie our truest feelings about people and the special community we call "our work." We need to be consistent and vigilant in eradicating hierarchical language and its many trappings within our companies, or we will surely discount and discourage our most important asset—our team!

Compensation—Of course, the whole issue of changing positions, which can imply a new title, and even a job with broader responsibility (although the person hasn't proven they can do it, yet) brings with it the traditional questions of compensation management. Although I would not consider myself a compensation expert, I have been privileged to observe many systems in many companies. My first real exposure to a compensation management system was an inadvertent one when I was still working for a large company. When I arrived at work one day, one of my friends who was always an enthusiastic fellow was particularly excited. With only a little prompting from me, he gladly shared with me that he had been notified that he had received a promotion. I congratulated him and asked where he would be going and what he would be doing. He reassured me that he was going nowhere, he was staying in our group, and he would still be assigned the same responsibilities. As a new and inexperienced employee, I admit I didn't understand his excitement, but I congratulated him and went to my desk.

The fellow who sat next to me that day was in an obviously poor mood. I asked him what was going on, and he told me that he was really discouraged because, pointing out my other friend who was so happy, he said, "You've probably heard it already, but he got my promotion." I asked if there was only one available, and he told me no, but that this would surely delay his promotion. I asked him, as I had asked my other friend, where do you want to be promoted and what would you do that you are not doing? He looked at me like I was from another planet and assured me that he, too, would be staying in our department, doing exactly what he had been doing, but he would not have the promotion to go along with it.

Thankfully, I had been assigned to a mentor within the department, so I asked him about this mysterious behavior of my two friends. He laughed at my naïve confusion, and then proceeded to explain that a promotion was very significant because it meant that there was the potential to make more money with each successively higher level. In other words, and here is where the understanding began to click for me, compensation was formally and directly tied to job titles, making promotions highly coveted for their economic gain.

As a purely technical person at the time, the more I thought about that explanation, the more I thought that system made little sense. In fact, in order to get beyond a senior technical position and pay grade, it was mandatory in our compensation system to have the word *Manager* in your title. Inherently, the compensation system dictated that no purely technical person could ever make as much as a manager. The consequence of this system was to routinely take some of our best engineers and encourage them to become managers in spite of their lack of managerial skills or aptitudes. Inevitably, they became some of our worst managers, which was incredibly frustrating for them. However, because of how painful it would be both socially and economically to accept a "demotion" in title and pay, they generally left the company after a couple of very frustrating years in "management" and we lost their intellectual capital to a competitor.

I have become a strong advocate of broad-banded compensation ranges. As with any compensation system, there is a need to balance market equity with internal equity. Every company will have different levels of sophistication in their compensation management processes, but we have done a thorough analysis for all of our specific jobs, assigning points to the various job elements identified, and matched those jobs to externally comparable jobs in our market. We then survey the market so that we can track starting salaries as well as what the impact of experience does to those salaries. Once we understand what the range of compensation is in the general market, we set a broad-banded compensation range that typically allows for up to 150 percent of the widest range we find in the market. Practically, this assures that our ranges for supervisors as well as technical personnel are competitive with the market while leaving us room to insure internal equity as well. After all, the supervisor with three years of total experience may not actually contribute at the level of our senior technical staff—either as a supervisor or as a technician themselves. It is very normal in our organization to find supervisors who make less money than the people they supervise. That just seems "right" to us.

Given that's how our system works, it is not necessarily true that accepting a "change of assignment" into a supervisory role will automatically be accompanied with a pay raise. Over time, with proven performance, it will happen. In this manner, technical workers are free to try their skills at supervision. As stated earlier, if the supervisory role does not work out well, the person is free to accept another "change of assignment" back into their non-supervisory role with no economic ramifications. This part of our system is an important element of maintaining internal equity, and in our industry, it helps to insure that we are not losing our intellectual capital by motivating career movement in a direction inconsistent with a person's fundamental gifts, talents, and abilities.

<u>Recruiting and Selection</u>—Peter Drucker once said that as managers we only really have four tools: selection (who we hire), assignment (where we play them), meetings, and reports. It seems to me that those are in the order of managerial leverage, too, with selection being the highest leverage activity we do and reports the lowest. Every company will eventually become whomever it selects. It's almost impossible to imagine placing too much emphasis on the importance of recruiting and selection. Whatever system you use, be diligent. Our first system for selection evolved from the observation that my batting average on selecting new personnel was better than everyone else in the company who had done selection. So, I inherited the "gatekeeper" function, and every new employee ultimately was interviewed by me. Everyone who has ever interviewed has their own set of questions that they enjoy asking, and I am no different. If my interviewing style was unique, it may have been because there was less of a focus on skills, and more of a focus on aptitudes and things the candidates thoroughly enjoyed doing. I was definitely more interested in character than competency in the interviewing process. If someone has appropriate aptitudes, we can train skills. But character runs much deeper and is infinitely harder to train. When the company's needs outgrew the cycles I had to devote to recruiting, we carefully selected another "gatekeeper" who had demonstrated a good track record while working with me. Today, it is a fairly grueling process to get hired from the candidate's perspective. They will be involved in multiple interviews with multiple persons before a final recommendation is made. It takes many hours of our team's time to get the next, right person for the team. But this careful approach and attention to the integrity of the corporate culture has given us an historical turnover rate of between 3 and 3.5 percent in an industry where double-digit rates are the norm. We believe it gives us a tremendous competitive advantage, and a long-term bank of intellectual assets that are unrivaled in our industry.

<u>Profit Sharing</u>—It began with a simple commitment to share the fruits of the labor with those who were most directly involved in

creating the fruit. On a quarterly basis, we have a gain-sharing program that pays a substantial percentage of each dollar above a budgeted threshold into a pool that is shared by all employees on a pro-rata basis based upon compensation dollars in the quarter. In theory, the relative contributions, both short-term and long-term, are built into individual compensation, making the allocation both fair and reasonable. It is a gain-sharing plan, so if we don't achieve the threshold performance, there is no additional expense, but if we exceed it, we reward it. By itself, this may not seem unusual. However, what might make it unusual is that this plan sits on top of a long-term profit-sharing plan that is an Equity Appreciation Plan. This plan is similar to an ESOP or "phantom stock" plan in that it allows employees to participate directly in the equity growth of the company over time. So there is a short-term (quarterly) cash component of our profit-sharing plan and a longer-term plan that shares growth in equity with the team that is creating that value. In the long-term plan, the employees get compensated just like investors, which encourages our team to think and act like they own the company because, in fact, they do!

Front-line Decision Making—Sometimes our newer supervisors will feel a bit overwhelmed by what it requires to manage in this professional, fully empowered environment. Having been asked many times for some guidelines, I finally relented and wrote down a few "things to tolerate" and "things not to tolerate." Feel free to use them if they are helpful to you! Here's the table—explanation to follow. . .

THINGS TO TOLERATE	THINGS NOT TO TOLERATE
Honest mistakes	Dishonesty
New ways of doing things	Disrespect
Youthful arrogance (to a point!)	Prima donnas
	Thoughtlessness

If our organization does not tolerate honest mistakes and new ways of doing things, we will crush the creativity and innovation out of the company. There is nothing more frustrating than to bring a new idea to the table only to hear, "we don't do it that way here." Frankly, if someone is actually innovating, many of those ideas will not work and will appear as mistakes. Celebrate them! Enjoy them! Don't repeat them, but do appreciate that someone is trying to make things better! This is one of the reasons that I encourage all of us to tolerate a fair dosage of youthful arrogance. As frustrating as it can be, it is mostly just immaturity, and frankly, the verve and edge that come from it can move the organization more quickly and more positively than most of us would care to admit.

There are, naturally, limits to each of these things we should tolerate. The limit of honest mistakes is dishonesty. Honest mistakes are often sins of commission—we tried to do something and it didn't work, but at least we were trying something! Dishonesty is a cancer to any organization and cannot be tolerated. It is insidious in that it comes in so many forms. It may not always be grounds for immediate dismissal, but it is the only thing for which I have executed an immediate dismissal in my entire career. By the way, it is still "in the other person's best, long-term interest" to not tolerate dishonesty. It may be a difficult way to learn the lesson (assuming they lose their job), but it's one of life's most important lessons.

The limit of tolerating new ways of doing things is when there is a lack of respect or appreciation for the people and/or processes that have been put in place to protect us and our clients. In our specific business, we have the keys to our clients' businesses in our hands by virtue of the access that we hold to their computer systems and data. We have established important safeguards to protect both us and our customers. It won't be acceptable to disrespect those processes even if we're doing something a new way. By the way, disrespect will typically evidence itself in many ways, not just one. This one is normally easy to spot.

Finally, the limit to tolerating youthful arrogance is when we are dealing with a prima donna (discussed earlier) or when the arrogance gives way to thoughtless or careless actions. Quite often, when a person is guilty of a thoughtless act, especially when they realize that we will tolerate an honest mistake, they will likely report that "they didn't mean to do it." When I hear that, I am reminded of what I used to tell my young children when a careless mistake had led them to be hurt or to hurt someone else. I explained to them that there are some things that are so important that it's not enough to "not mean to"—we must "mean not to" do the things that have the potential for disaster. It was true for my kids, and it's true for us as adults!

Staff Communication—Referring to Drucker's four basic managerial tools, we should talk about the effective use of meetings and reports. Regularly scheduled staff communication meetings and reports are very important to engaging our staff fully. If we want everyone to treat the company as though it was their own, and to work diligently to promote the company's success, it is only reasonable that we share with them on a regular basis how the company is doing. As a profit-sharing company, I believe that implies financial reporting transparency. As a leader trying to engage the whole person in the company's activities every day, I think it is important to use these regularly scheduled meetings as a "bully pulpit" to solicit support for the company's goals. Over the years, I have discovered that the biggest reason that people are not excited about all the great things going on in their company is that they simply don't know about them. Meetings and reports are really important tools to make sure that the entire team remains informed and engaged as we take on our world!

Cultural Events—In addition to regularly scheduled meetings and reports, every company has the opportunity to be creative with special cultural events throughout the year. These can range from big projects to informal luncheons. It's very common for us to have several cookouts during the summer when picnic weather is the rule. The company may buy the meat for volunteer chefs to serve their teammates over a lunch hour. In addition to a big push for United Way, our team will decide to raise money for numerous worthwhile causes throughout the course of a year, sometimes raising just money, but often bringing in purchased groceries or dry goods, depending on the cause being supported. A truly unique project at our company has evolved over several years that we call simply our "Heritage Wall." The Heritage Wall was initiated because Ron and I both felt a need to find an appropriate way to say "thank you" to our parents who were all very supportive as we started the new business. One of our principles for activities like this is that if we do it for one person, we want to make sure our method of recognition is available to the entire team. Until we moved into our campus facility a few years ago, no idea had seemed workable. But in this new facility, we had some very large walls on which we determined we could make this project work. Basically, we invite people to bring in pictures of their parents so that we may honor them by placing their photos on our Heritage Wall. Each time we update the wall, which is typically every eighteen months or so, we invite the parents who are being honored as well as any guests who might be interested in this proceeding, and we offer them an open house with a brief dedication and appreciation ceremony where we unveil the updated Heritage Wall once again.

Unique? Absolutely!

Cool? Absolutely!

Special place to work? No doubt!

Get your culture established, and then truly ENJOY the process of celebrating what makes and keeps it a special place. This continues to be a source of personal satisfaction and corporate fulfillment for our entire team!

EPILOGUE:

TRANSFORMING WORK—
TRANSFORMING THE WORLD

From the wonderful perspective of leading a company from start-up in a garage to our current status of over 500 employees with offices in three states, a national client base and best-in-class reputation for products and services, I am always a bit surprised with a fundamental response I receive from people who are introduced to our culture for the first time. Inevitably, there is an initial reaction that I can only characterize as skeptical. It's as though they are thinking, "Well, this might work for some companies, but it would never work for us."

What if I could demonstrate to you, my skeptical friends, that there is a direct correlation between running a business with this type of philosophy/corporate culture and financial performance? As I confessed earlier, we've always had an outside board of directors. Very early in our existence, they challenged us to report to them on an annual basis our results compared to our peers. Their purpose had nothing to do with "proving" the efficacy of a culture. They were looking for metrics to which they could reasonably hold their then-young management team accountable. I share this information without any desire to brag or to build us up. (When I want to be humbled about our relative commercial success, I simply remind myself that Microsoft started only two years before us, and my ego balloon is popped.) However, when compared to our peers in vertical market software, for over 15 years we have been a consistent top quartile performer. It may not be conclusive evidence for some, but for us, it is confirmation that legitimizes our work culture. A corporate culture won't make up for a bad market or a bad plan, but the company's culture will define its response to the market, and a healthy culture shouldn't tolerate a bad plan. Here's how I would summarize the importance of all we have discussed, and the primary reason for any commercial success that we may have achieved in the past or will achieve in the future:

Our uniquely sustainable competitive advantage *is* our corporate culture.

After all, when we started our business, we didn't start a country club. Our town already has one of those, and it's a good one. We started a software company, and any enterprise, whether for-profit or not-for-profit, needs to perform financially. We simply believe that financial performance is a by-product of great people doing a great job. Playing the game looking at the scoreboard is a sure strategy for losing the game! We're playing to win, and we invite you to join us on the journey!

Many of my early experiences of work were depressing and distressing. Does all work "feel" like this? For what purpose are the great masses of people exchanging their lives? The workplace needs transformation, my friends, and the experiment that I have shared with you is one place where the transformation is occurring. Will you join us? Together, we can change the world of work, one person at a time!